BROKEN WINGS

ISBN 978-1-0980-7410-4 (paperback)
ISBN 978-1-0980-7411-1 (digital)

Christian Faith Publishing, Inc.
832 Park Avenue
Meadville, PA 16335
www.christianfaithpublishing.com

Printed in the United States of America

BROKEN WINGS

So that his brief, innocent life might have
meaning for him and for those who followed,
his young mother bravely fought *the system*
all the way up to The White House.

Based on a True Story

Marge Glider

with

Gail Georgio

Marjorie Glider

Prologue

What If?

I woke up with a smile on my face this morning. What an incredible honor and proud moment; I'm so excited to be a part of my grandson's college graduation. Being a mom was always my dream and raising a wonderful daughter was my privilege, but being a grandmother is a joy unto itself. It is something that you can't imagine when you are young and first married.

Sharing in the accomplishments of my grandsons is so rewarding and keeps my heart full. But, as I drive to share this special day with my family, my mind wanders to times past, and I can't help but wonder "What if?"

What would my son have been like "if" he had had the chance of a normal life? What would our family have been like "if" we had been a typical, ordinary family? Once again, that is something you never think to imagine when you are preparing for your first baby.

As I watch the lines on the highway go past me, I am absorbed into memories from long ago, and I am drawn into reflections that I haven't let myself go to in a very long time. Not because I don't want to remember, but because after all of these years, the pain still feels incredibly real, almost like it happened yesterday. It carries me back to a day in November and the beginning of my story. A story like one that I never imagined would have been mine to tell.

"And they lived happily ever after." That is what I grew up believing in as I always loved romantic fairy tales.

My father moved our family eight times during my school years, so I was always the new kid in school. I hated it! There was no reason, just his whim to move. He had been an abandoned orphan, so there were no family ties to hold him anywhere.

When I finally went to college, four years of stability in my life seemed wonderful. My father decided early in his life that all his children would go to Florida Southern College in Lakeland, Florida, as it represented the goal of achieving a high status in life, in his mind. It was a beautiful, small Methodist college which had been designed by the famous architect, Frank Lloyd Wright.

I thrived in college as I became president of my sorority and a member of several scholastic societies. It was there that I met my prince charming, Dennis Glider. He was a year ahead of me and was in the Army ROTC program so he was going into the service upon graduation. We planned to marry after I graduated, the following June. However, the Berlin Wall went up, and world tensions ran high. There were fears that Russia was going to attack. So after he returned from basic training, he told me that we needed to get married the next weekend, as he was being shipped to Germany and did not know when he would return. That was only one week away!

I was still in my senior year and in the middle of midterm exams, so I panicked and said NO! But one week later, I was walking down the aisle in a beautiful wedding gown with all of our college friends in attendance. I was scared to death! Little did I know that the first obstacle in our life, which we considered to be a huge mountain, would turn out to be a small bump in the road compared to what life was going to throw at us.

*****

A mother's memory of her five-year-old son

"MOMMY, GUESS WHAT I FINDED OUT TODAY?"
"What, Barry?"
"I FINDED OUT THAT GOLDFISHES DON'T LIKE TO PLAY IN SANDBOXES."

1

The Waiting

Life is made up of many changes; and no state, be
it bright or clouded, will always continue.

—Spurgeon

The roar of the ocean as it intermingled with the sounds of seagulls
in search of food was intoxicating. In the distance, she could see a
young mahogany-tanned couple holding hands. Their lean bodies
seemed to dance in step with occasional bursts of laughter. These
sounds raised Marge's senses to a higher level of listening, and because
it was autumn and most tourists were gone, she felt more capable of
being *in tune* with a larger reality.

Breathing in the sea air made her feel new, fresh, and less cum-
bersome—a temporary clumsiness due to the child she was carrying. She walked closer to the ocean, savoring private and gentle
thoughts—uncomplicated reflections that snuggled softly inside the
edges of her mind: She and Denny, upon awakening that morning,
had decided not to immediately arise, his foot touching hers, his
voice, still blurry with sleep, asking, "Would you like me to make
breakfast this morning?"

"Mmmm. That sounds nice. Except I'm not hungry."

His expression had been one of rakish alarm. "My little Mommy
is *not* hungry this morning?"

Comfortable with the knowledge that she would not always be fat, she shot him a cocky glance as she placed her feet heavily on the floor. "No, I'm not hungry, but I do feel more energetic. In fact, I've decided to go for an early-morning walk by the ocean."

Lazily following her lead, Denny struggled out of bed. His handsome face, tanned golden by the warm Florida sun, smiled as he said, "I think I will go with you since the baby is due any time."

"This shirt will look nice with your navy blazer," she advised as she deliberately changed the subject.

"Marge…"

"A brisk walk will do me good. It's wonderful that your parents have opened their home to us until ours is ready, but I need a few hours to myself. Besides, after Barry's born, it might be a long time before I'll have this luxury."

"*Barry?* Barry might be a girl."

The name "Barry" already sounded familiar. She shook her head with confidence. "I know *who* I'm carrying. Barry is a beautiful blue-eyed little boy. You'll see. I've known from day one that our first child would be a boy."

The couple in the distance laughed again, reminding Marge that Denny and she were also young. Somehow this sudden shift into parenthood had made her feel older, wiser, and less concerned with "self." Life was no longer carte blanche but was instead a menu of carefully made choices. Her mind again backtracked to earlier that morning: the condensed moisture of an early dew had brought a silvery shimmer to the large palmetto leaves swaying outside her bedroom window. Despite having lived most of her life in Florida, she had never tired of its pleasant climate, abundant sunshine, and beautiful scenery. The sweet smells of various blossoms sent a perfume over a quiet earth, automatically filling her with ease.

She had traveled much of Florida's east coast, which was protected by narrow sandbars and inlets, and when traveling inland, she often followed the pine and palmetto flatlands that stretched from the Georgia border to Florida's southern tip. Warmed by the surrounding subtropical waters of the Atlantic Ocean of the east and by the Gulf of Mexico on the west, it was no wonder Ponce de León had thought Florida to be an island.

This particular morning, south Florida was cooler than normal. While autumn in the north was teased by early frosts, it had yet to come to Florida's beaches. And while watching the wind blow the waves to and from shore, it was also a time to remove the tiny wrinkles that life often brought.

The ocean, no matter how calm, always commanded attention. Today, however, the life she carried within commanded attention as did the completion of their first home. Daily she mentally decorated its yet unfinished rooms, but since money was tight, this decorating was more of a dream than a reality. Still, dreams did not in themselves come with price tags. Dreams rode on the wings of a smile and soared on the wings of hope. Dreams were not merely illusions but rather the touchstones of existence.

Dreams kept life imaginatively wonderful and made the impossible *possible*.

Although only in their early twenties, she and Denny had woven their dreams from a life fabric that was both strong and enduring. Despite becoming parents while still financially strapped, despite accepting a hand-me-down crib for Barry's nursery, in the final analysis, this did not matter. Their baby was not secondhand.

He would be new and pure and perfect.

Subdued, her thoughts took on the role of a shadow-puppet play that was staged with her as its director: *her* marriage would be different from her parents' in the sense she would be a full partner, not a subordinate. After all, this was 1963. Her mother had been a product of an era where many women served and obeyed their husbands, where they looked the other way, where they dared not "make waves." Having grown up in a household where the laws of nature were unbalanced, where she and her younger brother, Jim, often lamented that there was *only* one law—*their father's law*—she had promised that once she married, it would be different. She would be an equal. It was while in her freshman year at Florida Southern, after a fraternity drove over to pick up her sorority for a social, that she saw Dennis Glider for the first time. She knew something special was about to happen. Handsome, charming, and undeniably masculine, he was totally unlike her father; and more, he was different from anyone else she had met. An expression in his eyes stated he had his own truth and dreams to achieve in his own way.

He was a man with goals. However, they did not connect again until two years later.

In retrospect, their courtship was uncluttered, almost "invented" because of its Cinderella-like setting. But then love seldom came when one looked for it. When it did, it was right on time.

With Denny, she felt a freedom never experienced before. She was able to not only laugh freely but also to express self-designed opinions that had been denied her by her father. Rather than existence being a conflict as it had for most of her life, there existed a mutual respect. Denny was so accepting of *who* she was and *how* she thought that they were able to discuss anything and everything. Of course, being in love colored her life with a vibrancy that may have condoned an unrealistic type of thinking. On another level, the responsibility of being in love and planning a future together had made them shed the first layers of their youth, yet not enough to make the future less bright or less exciting.

Being a part of Denny's life was as if a veil had been lifted.

The following June, after Denny's graduation, they became engaged, with plans to marry after she graduated a year later. Because of the Berlin crisis, Denny entered the Army that fall, and after two months of basic training at Fort Sill in Oklahoma, he returned to Florida on leave. She met him at the plane. "Marge, I'm going to be sent to Germany. I don't know when I'll return," he said softly. "I'd like us to get married next weekend."

"*Next* weekend?"

Denny nodded. His blue eyes shone with confidence as he pulled her into his arms. "Yes. I love you…"

Stunned by this sudden turn of events, she had grown quiet and reflective. Somehow the less he said, the more she listened. On the other hand, acting impulsively had never been part of her nature. "No, I can't!" she pleaded. "I mean, Denny…!"

"Will you at least think about it?" he pleaded.

Promising him she would at least *think* about it, she talked it over with a friend. "If I were you," her friend advised, "I'd marry him."

"You mean *now?*"

"Why not *now?* You're of age. I wouldn't chance losing someone like Dennis Glider."

"But I'm in the middle of midterm exams—"

"And Denny's in the middle of a midworld crisis. If he's not afraid to go overseas, how can you be afraid to marry someone you love?"

She did love Denny; she also admired his fearless acceptance of meeting life head on. Of course, they were lucky enough to be living in an age of a youthful president who was receiving credit for restoring optimism to America and whose glamorous wife was an *equal* companion. Even though she and Denny were not particularly fond of the politics of President John F. Kennedy, she could not help but respect a certain daringness that now pervaded. This president and his wife were a moving force behind a new type of thinking where compromise was not necessarily a strength and where outward vulnerability was not necessarily a weakness.

She married Denny.

Like their courtship, her marriage to Denny had become a colorful extension of its fairy-tale conception. Like any fairy tale, there were times when the carriage remained a pumpkin, yet in the final analysis, the ride was more smooth than bumpy; and for all purposes, the glass slipper had remained safe and intact.

A sand-washed shell caught her attention, bringing her back to the moment where she walked the beach carrying Denny's son. She bent and picked up a shell, turning it gently in her hand. Because it was so interesting, she decided to add it to her collection. She put it in the pocket of her smock and continued her walk, reminding herself of how perfect her life had become and would always be.

Breathing in deeply, she counted her blessings. She would remember today forever, and although impatient for Barry's arrival, she wanted to prolong this particular moment. She was smitten by everything large and small. She felt strong and durable and ageless and seasonless.

Nothing could or would ever crush her.

As the peaceful rhythm of the ocean broke against the shore, it occurred to her that the sea was like some mystical clock that measured off life one second at a time—always ticking, always measuring, always eternal.

To avoid the sting of sand that a sudden easterly wind blew in her eyes, she turned toward a sheltered area where several dunes sat rigid in their posture. As she neared the dunes, she noted the remains of a sandcastle. Bending, she tried to repair its south wall, but it was too far gone. It would take more time to repair than to rebuild. She didn't know exactly why, but she felt sad when thinking this. Oh, well…

Standing, she withdrew crumbs of bread from her pocket and tossed them in the air. Seemingly from out of nowhere, a dozen gray seagulls swept down, grabbed the crumbs one swoop at a time, sailed off, and were gone, almost as though they had never existed.

Once again, she grew reflective as she compared the sea and its energy to the rhythm of life. Suddenly she felt a slight movement in her abdomen. Tilting her head back, she smiled. "Barry! You moved!"

At least she *thought* Barry had moved.

Marge waited for another movement. When it did not come, she rubbed her hand gently over the area where Barry slept before his entry into life. It never occurred to her that it was unusual for a baby *not* to kick inside the womb. Because it was her first pregnancy, she had nothing to compare it with, and thus there was no alarm.

After the wind died, she walked back to the water's edge and, despite the damp sand, lumbered into a seating position. Trying to arrange her bulky body into a comfortable stance, she kicked off her sandals and stretched out her legs, allowing the snow-white sea foam to tease her toes. The ocean did indeed symbolize life, yet she must also remember that despite the ocean's unrestrained, unchangeable motion, in reality, *she* was the navigator of her existence. God had given her the power and freedom to set her dreams in motion, to chart the course of her life.

And life *was* good. God had blessed her.

*****

A mother's memory of her five-year-old son

"MOMMY, GUESS WHAT I FINDED OUT TODAY?"

"What, Barry?"

"I FINDED OUT THAT IF YOU HIDE YOUR PEAS UNDER THE MASHED 'TATOES, YOU CAN'T TASTE 'EM."

2

Echoes of a Struggle

Bravery is being the only one who knows you're afraid.

—Franklin P. Jones

Dennis Glider paused outside his wife's hospital room. His body, tense and straight, leaned against a wall. His hands hung rigidly at his sides while his shoulder blades were drawn tightly together. Turning slightly, he watched the sunlight of early-morning stream through a window at the end of the hospital corridor. He thought of how brilliant the institutional walls looked in the fragile light of a new day and thought also of how fragile dreams were.

Biting his lower lip and shaking his head, Dennis walked slowly down the long sterile halls, down the stairs, through the admission's lobby and outside. There were a myriad of feelings pulsating through his body, and until now, he had never learned the process of sorting them out. One conclusion had already been reached: *the days ahead would be difficult.* He would have to be strong, not only because he was a husband and now a father but also because a law of nature demanded that the male of the species *be* strong.

Before walking to his car, he turned and, in the stillness of morning, looked back at the hospital. The stone of the building glowed in the sun's rays, yet the granite also appeared cold and unmovable. Without wanting to think further, he walked swiftly away from the sun and to his car. He needed an immediate sense of motion to ease his distress.

Driving down roads that led past various-shaped houses, he passed a church where stained-glass windows glittered in the sun, then turned down another street where lace curtains floated through an open window of a small home. A few feet away, a large dog rummaged through an overturned trash can. Another type of motion caused him to slow his car. It was a line of diapers fluttering in the breeze between two houses.

Marge wondered *why* Denny had shown so little emotion when she felt so much? Was he oblivious to her suffering? He had stood by her bed saying little yet, as was his habit with people, looked straight at her. His calm demeanor should have been welcomed, yet for once, she wanted some deep emotion from him; for once, she wanted to see him as afraid as she was. She could give no valid reason for the sudden resentment she felt. All she knew was that instead of seeing a man capable of great strength, she saw a man who seemed incapable of great sympathy.

She shook her head sadly. It was a new morning; there was much to be done. November 7, 1963, was a date that would forever be the birthday of their first son, Barry Eugene Glider. He was a beautiful blond-haired, blue-eyed angel who had floated into their lives almost effortlessly.

If *only*…

Again she shook her head as though to do so would negate the meaning of "*if only.*"

The night before Barry's birth was without incident. After retiring for the evening, she was awakened shortly after midnight when her water broke. That was one time when Denny appeared rattled, but he quickly regained composure and called Dr. Gallagher, who said he would meet them at the hospital in about an hour.

"But what if the baby comes sooner?" Denny had asked with apprehension.

Dr. Gallagher had laughed. "The first one usually takes a while. Get packed, drive slow. You've plenty of time."

Denny drove faster than normal as he feared the doctor might be wrong. Dr. Gallagher was correct and told Denny to go home and rest. "It will be hours before the baby's born," he had explained with a slight smile. Denny started to protest. "There's no use pacing and worrying. Everything's fine, Dennis. I'll call you when we're ready to take Marge into the delivery room."

Marge had not been awake for the actual birth but knew as soon as consciousness began that "it" was over. "What did we have?" she asked groggily.

Dr. Gallagher's eyes had suddenly clouded over as he cleared his throat. "You and Dennis have a son."

Trying to further outdistance the dreaminess still enveloping her, her hands had touched the area of her empty womb. A son!

Barry had been born! Thank you, God!

Her eyes grew less foggy and more focused as they fixed upon the doctor. Something in the way he avoided eye contact made her uncomfortable. "What time is it?" she asked.

"Early morning."

"Where is my baby? Can I hold him?"

"Of course, you can," Dr. Gallagher replied quietly, "as soon as Dennis arrives." That was a strange statement.

Marge nodded as though she understood. She tried to smile because it seemed this was a time to smile. After all, she and Denny were now parents. Together they had created a child, and it seemed fitting that they should be together when they viewed Barry for the first time. Therefore, Dr. Gallagher's suggestion made sense.

Then why was she suddenly so *afraid?*

When Denny entered the room, his eyes immediately locked with Dr. Gallagher's. Noting this, Marge knew there was another reason *why* Dr. Gallagher wanted Denny there. Remaining quiet, she watched the two men curiously. Something puzzled her about their manner. Having grown accustomed to *not* always making her voice heard, she waited to be *included* in whatever drama was taking place. Instinctively she sensed that they knew something she didn't.

"Marge," Dr. Gallagher began, then stopped as he looked over at Denny.

"For heaven's sake," Marge chastised, "*what* is wrong? Is Barry okay?"

Dr. Gallagher was relieved by Marge's annoyance. "Yes, and no," he replied evenly. He drew a chair close, then sat. "Your son was born with severe club feet."

Before she had time to ask questions, Barry was brought to her. Marge felt her world explode as she looked at her beautiful baby son with his left leg raised upward, and like a broken rubber band, his right foot laying helplessly on the calf of his right leg. Her head began to reel as the deluge of Barry's problem hit her. She looked to Denny for comfort.

"We've called in Dr. Forrester," Denny said in a calming voice. "He's the best orthopedic specialist in Miami."

"A baby's bones are very soft," Dr. Gallagher added. "Dr. Forrester will be putting Barry's legs in casts either today or tomorrow."

"Does that mean Barry will eventually walk?" Marge asked hopefully.

"It's too early to tell," Dr. Gallagher explained. "The casts will go all the way up to his body. Hopefully, a correction of the legs and feet will be made. As I said, a baby's bones are very soft, very moldable."

Marge felt her hands shake. She could not help but question how they would pay for any of this? They had no insurance because Denny had started a new job with a marketing firm. What little financial reserve they had had gone toward their new home. They had even borrowed a small amount from Denny's grandmother to make up the difference needed for a down payment.

Through all of this, Barry's eyes remained closed in sleep.

Slowly they opened wide. They were a clear blue, and in the noisy confusion of her terror, her newborn's eyes spoke of something that needed no remolding—*LOVE*.

As he continued driving up one street and down another, Denny thought how off-balance life sometimes was. It seemed that only yesterday his primary concern had been the starting of a new career and the purchase of a new home, microscopic challenges compared to the problems now faced or rather the problems his son faced. He recalled the many questions that had invaded his thoughts when Marge had told him about the pregnancy: Would the baby be a boy or a girl? Would Marge's pregnancy be without complication? Could they afford to bring a child into the world? Would his career growth coincide with the growth of a child to adulthood? Knowing that he would be leaving the Army, he had updated his resume; and although he had no job skills, he was counting upon the fact that a college degree in business management and marketing, together with self-assurance, would be enough to impress a perspective employer. Although stationed in Fort Lewis, Washington, they had decided that this new adventure would be better served in Florida.

"'Let's drive across country and camp along the way," Marge had suggested. "We can experience the wonders of the land before permanently settling down."

"That's a three-thousand-mile hike. Will you be up to it?" Marge had thrown back her head and laughed.

"Why wouldn't I? Having a baby is natural. It happens every day of the year. It'll be fun and relaxing. What could possibly go wrong?"

After the nurse returned Barry to the nursery, Marge attempted to will strength into her body—the type of strength that seemed to come naturally to men. They were better equipped at keeping their emotions in check. What she did not understand was that this difference was an important distinction that separated a woman from a man—that without these emotional levels, the entire human race might find itself living in a void of feelings.

A few voices sounded sleepily from the dark porches of her memory: one was the sound of her father's stern voice as he scolded her and her brother or as he addressed her mother in a dictatorial tone. In an attempt to understand the first man who had played an important role in her life, she quietly replayed what she knew about her father, as though to understand George Jackson might provide shelter from a storm already growing in force.

Born an only child in 1918 in Florida, two weeks after his birth, the flu epidemic killed his mother. His father, Henry, devastated and helpless, did his best to keep George; but when sole parenting became impossible, he climbed into his horse-drawn wagon and took his two-week-old-son to his brother's home.

Henry gave his son away and was never heard from again.

Because times were hard, baby George was passed from one relative to another until an aunt and uncle—out of duty rather than love—permanently took him in. George Jackson, although not a physical orphan, was a spiritual orphan. At seventeen, with his rebellious spirit somewhat settled, he met and married a shy farm girl of twenty-one, Marge's mother, Alma. The frequent rages her father had displayed toward his docile wife, and eventual son and daughter, were undoubtedly the result of a child crying out in frustration for love. Never truly belonging and thus having lost control as a child, his need to control as an adult was overwhelming. While her gentle and kind mother stood silent in this marriage of domination, Marge viewed her parents' relationship with an incredulity that grew into quiet outrage. Her father's cruel tongue and need to control filled her with an anguish that was compounded by grief, despair, and desolation. Now, herself a married woman, she was beginning to understand that nothing significant had changed from one generation to another. She only wanted it to, and although the cloth was new, the pattern was a repeat. In her desire to keep peace and to make her husband happy, she had begun to keep her inner feelings and fears to herself. This had become more apparent whenever she and Denny quarreled. Rather than taking a firm position, she would run.

Literally.

She recalled one time running to a park and sitting upon a swing until dark. She always returned home to Denny—a motion that suggested an argument had been settled. In truth, for the sake of peace and a desire to please, issues remained unstated until buried beneath other issues of like nature. She wondered what would happen if ever she were to peel away all those thin layers that were building, one upon the other?

As noiseless sobs shook Marge's body and tightened her throat, hot tears ran down her cheeks. She looked through their wetness at the woman in the hospital bed next to her. Knowing her name was Betty Jo, Marge wondered why this strange woman—tall and thin with scraggly brown hair—had remained quiet and somewhat distant.

Seeing Marge's tears caused Betty Jo to speak, and when she did, her voice was soothing and beautiful. "I have four children at home," she told Marge.

"Then this new baby is number five?" Marge asked politely.

"I'm not here for having given birth," Betty Jo responded in that amazing voice. "I'm here for exhaustion."

Just as Barry's lack of kicking within the womb had not been viewed as unusual, it did not occur to Marge that Betty Jo's "rest" in a maternity room was equally unusual. She was so caught up in her own problems that she did not notice that Betty Jo received no telephone calls or visitors. That realization would come later.

Instead, she felt her body relax and her hands unclench as she listened to Betty Jo speak.

"I have a son who's retarded," Betty Jo said calmly.

Marge let out a deep gasp as she realized how lucky she and Denny were. After all, their son had a good chance of being healed. And even if the worst occurred—that Barry might not walk—in all other ways, he was normal. "I'm sorry," Marge responded as she realized she was no longer afraid. Strangely Betty Jo's plight made her own less important. Instead she was horribly ashamed that she had wallowed in her own grief. It was then she recalled something she once heard: "I was lamenting the fact I had no shoes until I met a man who had no feet."

Betty Jo smiled, and when she did, her face grew beautiful.

There was an intellectual strength in her dark eyes, and as her thin body appeared to fill with light, her worn hands seemed lineless and pure, almost like a baby's. "Don't be sorry," Betty Jo told Marge. "This child has brought me greater joy than any of the others. Whenever life seems hopeless, all I do is look in my son's eyes, and I find strength and beauty. These children are God's special angels."

For a moment Marge wished she possessed the power to rectify this injustice—to mend a human error—but then it occurred to her that *all* children came from God and that *God never made a mistake.*

All children, no matter their shape or coloring, no matter their physical limitations, held the kind of beauty that mirrored eternity.

"Children, all children," Betty Jo added softly, "walk upon sacred ground."

The noise and confusion that had enveloped Marge's soul became wonderfully quiet. She heard the lapping of the far-off sea and remembered how it spoke of eternal life. And even when the beach was deserted and dreary, when the ocean was surrounded by fog, the fog always lifted. Turning her eyes fully upon Betty Jo, she stared at her curiously.

Looking like no one Marge had ever seen before but looking as familiar as a fading sunset—or a sudden beam from a lighthouse—Betty Jo seemed to have quietly appeared from out of the fog of nowhere.

*****

A mother's memory of her five-year-old son

"Mommy, guess what I finded out today?"

"What, Barry?"

"I finded out that if you kick some kid in the knee, he'll hit you with a stick."

3

Vagabond Memories

If faith can see every step of the way it is *not* faith.

—Barclay

"If you don't have a son, the Glider name will die on the vine," Denny's younger sister Kay had told him. That was the way it was meant to be, but sadly, gravity had reversed itself.

From his open car window, Denny looked at the palm trees, at the various stucco structures, and at the great rise of the sky beyond the flat horizon. His face held an expression of strained attentiveness. Inside he felt numb. He did not know whether this numbness was a surrender to pain or whether it was a type of physical veil that masked fear.

In the bright morning light, it seemed as if his entire "being" sighed. He turned down another anonymous street in order to allow the past to reconstruct in his mind. It had not been long ago when he and Marge had arrived back in Florida, she pregnant, he searching for his first job. He had quickly discovered the catch-22 regarding employment: everyone wanted those with experience, but how could experience be acquired if no one offered employment? Luck had been on his side. Through an employment agency, he had accepted a position as an account executive with an established market research firm in the Miami area. He took pride in viewing life as if it were a game with a reachable goal. How one reached that goal was not as important as actually getting into the game and playing. He felt that rather than waiting for a hole in the defense to open, it was better to create that "hole."

Developing these types of philosophies made life simple and comfortable. Life did not have to consist of waving colorful banners or dancing in the end zone when a touchdown was made. But then life was not meant to "bench-sit" through either. Life was like a door waiting to be opened, and as was his way, he never simply knocked; he sought to find the right keys. One key was bound to unlock even the most secure door. The word *no* translated to "If this way doesn't work, let's keep searching until we find a way that does work."

Today he felt as though he were locked outside a thousand dark castles surrounded by dangerous moats, each moat mocking Marge's Cinderella-like outlook on life. Today he was unable to be her knight in shining armor.

Their "once upon a time" was coming to an end.

His growing-up years had been different than Marge's in the sense that rather than a strict home environment, he and his two sisters enjoyed an atmosphere where everyone worked together in the family's Miami hardware store. Since Marge had grown up in rural areas, she regarded him as a big city boy. He had jokingly told her that the city boy in him loved the beach. Whenever possible, he and the guys, especially his best friend Hal, would hit the seaside drive-ins, water ski, scuba dive, fish, then cruise the beach to wave and joke with the girls.

Work and responsibility had left time for fun.

He smiled as he remembered Hal, who in truth was more of a brother than a best friend. They attended the same college, and although spreading their wings in different directions, they had remained close, pledging to always be there for each other. Then came that particular night of their sophomore year's homecoming dance: he and Hal had planned to double date, but because Hal had been unable to get a date, he had offered Denny the use of his car. "Are you sure you won't need it?" Denny had asked.

"Nah. I'm going off with a friend who has a car. How about if I meet you at the frat house following the dance."

When Hal failed to show up after the dance, Denny went to bed. It wasn't until the next morning that he learned Hal and his friend had been killed when a train hit their car. The incompletion of Hal's life weighed heavily upon him, making him realize that it wasn't death that was to be feared per se, but the incompleteness of one's life—the unfulfillment of dreams. It was old men who should die, not the young whose life had only barely begun. On the personal level, he had thought, no more would Hal look him straight in the eyes to offer a dare; no more would they share a dozen summers together, teasing and taunting the world. As his list of "no mores" grew, Denny knew Hal would be with him in the way memories guided the future. He only wished today, now, in this present moment, he could talk to Hal and ask him what to do.

Thank God Marge had entered his life shortly after Hal's death. She was beautiful, serene, innocent, and sexy all at once. It was when she was not around that he had begun to realize how much he missed her, how much he wanted her to be waiting for him. As one memory spilled over onto another, many without obvious connection, he recalled how his sister Kay had complained of the constant kicking and movement her baby had made during pregnancy and how Marge never complained of this. The only discomfort Marge had suffered was an extremely painful spot between her breasts, which turned out to be where Barry's feet were pressing. Apparently, since Barry was almost nine pounds at birth, there was no more room for him to grow, and thus the club feet.

That was the reason for the club feet and the *only* reason. It had to be.

Denny's memories stopped as though something ordered him to replay his son's birth: After a few hours of sleep, he had rushed back to the hospital. Marge had already been sedated and had slept through the delivery. He had been the first to hold Barry, the first to see that *something* was terribly wrong. Nothing like that was supposed to happen, but it had, and he had to reassure Marge that the doctors would be able to straighten Barry's legs. Yet even as he recalled his words of hope, something vague and frightening made him tremble. Tears welled up in his eyes and fell down his cheeks. Once again, the thought of Hal passed through his mind, and he wondered *why* with the birth of new life had he suddenly thought of a life lost? Denny blinked, unprepared for the depth of this strange feeling. Because the feeling was so fleeting, it seemed best not to explore it.

The two women in the hospital talked so softly that the nurses passing by the open door could not hear their words. As Betty Jo spoke, Marge relaxed against her pillows and thought that although her suffering was real, listening to Betty Jo's calm, peaceful tones became like a candlelight flickering in the darkness.

Studying her roommate, Marge wondered if Betty Jo was as tired as she appeared? This strange woman also seemed so alone yet not lonely. What was it about her that was so out of place? Betty Jo did not look like anyone Marge had ever seen before. She was more of a throwback to something undefined, more of a *presence* that might forever be inexplicable.

At first all she had seen was a woman too thin, too worn, and a woman grown too old before her time. Originally, she had viewed Betty Jo as servile, one who swept floors and took orders. Now, as Marge listened to Betty Jo's voice as it gently rose and fell, and as she was drawn into Betty Jo's dark eyes, she saw a figure who was both timeless and regal.

Not only did Marge listen to Betty Jo's gentle words, but something deep inside wanted to know *what* was spoken. Marge did not understand even one quarter of what Betty Jo was saying, but there appeared a monumental truth in every word. Perhaps it was Denny's emotional withdrawal that made her respond to Betty Jo's complete ability to care. Without knowing exactly *why*, she began telling Betty Joe about herself. "When I was growing up, my father moved around quite a lot."

Betty Jo nodded in the gesture of asking Marge to continue.

"He was always a mechanic at Ford, no matter where we moved. He was very good at what he did even though he only had an eighth-grade education."

"Education is what remains when everything school-taught is forgotten," Betty Jo observed quietly.

"Daddy wanted my brother and I to be well-educated, to go to college. He felt that only through education can anyone realize total potential. He never wanted us to be victims of 'a mind wasted.' Education was the key to a successful chance at life."

Betty Jo nodded. "Education is useful, but remember, although education can train, it doesn't *create* intelligence. More importantly, intelligence is not always as it appears."

Marge's nod was more a polite reflex than one of understanding. "My father's word was law, and I always sought to please him, despite the fact I continually asked questions. This annoyed him to no end." Marge paused, then added, "Ironically, the main purpose of education is to bring people to the point of continual question asking."

Betty Jo's all-seeing eyes sparkled with an awareness that eluded Marge. "Most people do not ask the right questions," Betty Jo said.

"The *right* questions?" Marge asked.

"Continue…"

"And your plans for parenting?"

"I don't want to be like my father."

"Or your mother?"

Marge sighed. "I admire her loving qualities, but I don't want to take a backseat to my husband. She loved and feared Daddy. I think you can grow to hate what you fear."

"Do you hate your father?"

"No, just some of his qualities. He ruled by fear and a domination that was justified by his interpretation of love."

Betty Jo smiled sadly. "That's because your father was afraid."

"*Afraid?*"

"Anyone who uses tools of fear in order to control others is a person drowning in fear."

As Betty Jo continued to speak, her rich, deep voice grew distant. Listening to it relaxed Marge. She felt the tense muscles that had cramped her body letting go while a tender warmth embraced her being. The sensation of drifting off into a land of sleep took hold,

26

yet quite the opposite was happening to her mind. It was now more alert, more conscious. "I was so afraid every time we moved and I had to make new friends," Marge reflected after a moment of silence. "I attended school in a little farming town in southern Michigan from the eighth grade through the eleventh grade. The area and the people were wonderful, and we lived in a pre-Civil War fieldstone house. I ran around with a great group of kids and, of course, even had a serious boyfriend. Everything was going my way. I was to be on the yearbook staff my senior year, was selected by the faculty to be our school's representative at Boys' and Girls' State—a big honor—and my French teacher had chosen me to be an exchange student the following summer. I was an honor student." Marge looked down at her hands. "It should have been one of the happiest times of my life."

"And it wasn't?"

"No…my father…my accomplishments meant nothing. I never measured up."

Betty Jo pulled a single flower from a vase on the bedside table and smelled it, then began caressing its petals. "Were your accomplishments for you or to please your father?"

Marge felt the urge to listen closely to Betty Jo's question because in the question was the answer, or was it a message? "If I accomplished something," Marge almost whispered, "I might gain approval and acceptance."

Having acknowledged this, she would have to decipher whether *any* of her accomplishments were for herself or to please someone else? For now though, there was this tremendous desire to continue on with her original train of thought. It was as if she *needed* to get her past recorded as soon as possible in order to have time for what might lie in the future. "The economy was pretty bad, and Daddy had a good job, but when he got a notion in his head, nothing stood in his way—*the Gospel according to George.*"

Betty Jo laughed slightly but said nothing.

Marge stopped to review this particular memory. "Daddy got it into his head that my boyfriend Bob and I might elope. In truth, we planned to attend college and get married after we graduated. I think this was more talk than realism. Anyway, two weeks before beginning my senior year, Daddy sold the farm, and we moved to Ft. Myers, Florida. One year left to go and he did this to me."

"Why Florida?"

"I don't know. Daddy probably saw a postcard and we were from Florida. It was a repeated ritual that we moved ourselves. Mother and I were crammed inside a loaded car with a bird, a cat, and two goldfish. Daddy and Jim were in a truck that pulled a trailer loaded with two horses and two dogs. I was so upset that I cried around the clock. That's one of the few times my mother got mad at me. She was sick of my tears."

"Tears are always the most truthful emotion. Rather than a sign of weakness, they're often a cleansing for the soul."

"I stopped crying. We rented a nice house on the river, and Jim and I were once again the new kids on the block."

"This must have made you and your brother very close."

"He and I fought a lot growing up. The first day of school, I was lost in the halls, fighting back tears. My old school had a population of five hundred, while Ft. Myers had over two thousand students. Suddenly I saw a familiar face, and I was overjoyed to see my brother. So, yes, in one sense, we were close—counterparts in *aloneness* I guess."

"None of us are born to be alone," Betty Jo said with feeling. "Sometimes we choose our counterparts, other times they choose us."

"I tried to make friends, and I did pretty well. But my heart was breaking for the old and for Bob. I was determined to see him but didn't know how. I started skipping lunch to save money so I could buy a bus ticket back to Michigan over the Christmas holidays. I guess I was trying to run back to the safety of *what had been* rather than facing what was."

"It's a poor memory that only looks backward," Betty Jo reminded.

Marge continued to capture faint glimpses of *who* she was on the physical level. It also occurred to her that she might be trying to catch a glimpse of her inner being or, more accurately, to become aware of all sides of her spiritual nature. Whatever was happening, she knew she had to rid herself of a combination of past suffering and joy in order to be strong enough to carry new weights. There was a desperation attached to this that she could not figure out.

It was as if she were preparing herself for something, but *for what?*

*****

A mother's memory of her five-year-old son

"MOMMY, GUESS WHAT I FINDED OUT TODAY?"
"What, Barry?"
"I FINDED OUT THAT DOGS DON'T LIKE JELL-O."

4

Cinderella and Her Prince

I like the dreams of the future better than the history of the past.

—Jefferson

Marge could feel Betty Jo's eyes studying her with an understanding that filled her with strength. And that luminous voice! Even when Betty Jo was not speaking, her voice resonated with a distant echo. It was like a ripple of sunlight that spread long and clear and bright.

In this brief silence, Marge realized that Betty Jo *knew* what she was thinking. This temporary stranger somehow knew all her fears, knew that despite her deep love for Denny that uncertainties were pulling at her. Marge shook her head and breathed in deeply in an attempt to remember *where* she was.

She was in the hospital. She had given birth to Barry.

In the quiet of remembering, she could still feel the swell of their baby within her womb, feel the area where he had recently rested. This memory was shattered by self-blame: Had her body been too small to offer Barry enough room for growth? Had he sought to spread his growing limbs and could not, thus the club feet? With each exhale, she felt the fullness of her breasts, so ready with milk, press against her hospital gown. She wanted to go to Barry and hold him close, tell him how much she loved him. Instead, a wave of convulsing sobs broke over her.

It felt as if her soul were drowning.

"Separating thoughts from feelings is impossible," Betty Jo said.

Marge nodded, then swallowed. "I feel so afraid."

"When we're afraid, we often find it hard to hear our inner voice. We become like children in the dark, begging that someone else turn on the light so that no closet monster will devour us." Betty Jo eased her thin body into full seating position. "Can you imagine the caterpillar being afraid of entering its cocoon of darkness? Yet instinctively it knows the cocoon will eventually break open, and light will exist. In the end, by existing in temporary darkness, the caterpillar is greater than it was before. It's now the butterfly, and it's no longer confined to crawling but rather to the magic of soaring."

"The unknown is so frightening."

Betty Jo nodded. "Don't be afraid of your pain, Marge. Remember that pain can either destroy us or make us stronger."

The way the sun was streaming through the window gave Betty Jo's skin a translucent glow. For a moment Marge stared at this strange image, then turned her eyes downward, angry at herself for having wept. After all, the woman in the other bed had greater problems than she. Betty Jo's son was retarded. At least Barry's condition was temporary.

Ashamed that her vision was so narrow and selfish, she took another long breath to pacify her seesawing emotions. Gently she disengaged her hands, which were still embracing her now empty womb, then she thanked God that Barry *only* had club feet. After all, life could easily have gone the other way; she could be in Betty Jo's situation. "How old is your son?" Marge asked softly.

A smile of pure love lightened Betty Jo's dark eyes. "He's ten."

"Was he…born that way?"

Betty Jo smiled in a way that it appeared the sun rose in her eyes. "My son was born as he should have been born—a wonderful, spiritual being."

Slightly embarrassed, Marge felt her palms dampen. "Of course. I only meant—"

"It's all right, Marge. There's nothing wrong with your question. Believe that every child born is a creation of a Greater Power, not simply a physical result of the human body. *Every* child created—no matter what its station in life, no matter what its physical condition—has a special task and duty. What will happen *will* happen. All your fears and anxieties cannot change the past or even the present. But you do have the power to change the future. You're experiencing guilt over something you think you might have done or might *not* have done. You're looking for someone or something to blame. That's futile energy. After all, if you accidentally stub your toe, do you blame your toe or cut it off?"

Marge responded with a slight tilt of the head.

"We're all born for a purpose. My son has brought me such joy, peace, and happiness. Whenever a situation appears hopeless, I look into this child's eyes. Love and strength are always found. Children are born to share their light, and His, with us." Looking at the flower she still caressed, Betty Jo commented, "Just as nature creates each flower perfectly—one that exists for itself, not for applause or acceptance—God creates each soul perfectly. At this creation, each soul is indifferent to applause. A flower doesn't bloom because someone told it to. The wildflower doesn't *unbloom* because it fears someone will ridicule it or compare it with the cultured rose. It *is* because it *is*." Reaching over, Betty Jo handed Marge the flower. "This flower has its own scent and color. Its beauty is to be enjoyed as it is rather than what it *isn't*."

Marge absorbed the flower's special fragrance.

"Although my son's brain has not developed, his mind is well-formed because the mind is of the spirit, while the brain is of the physical. Since the mind is connected to a higher level, the spiritual level, it cannot be unprogressive. It knows no retardation. Like the massive oak, the soul has its roots in the eternal. It's strong and enduring. While my son's brain rests in a silence that is temporary, his mind is in perfect communication with God—with All-Truth and All-Knowledge."

Marge knew that her confusion was visible. "I wish I had your faith. I can't understand what God's purpose is in allowing *any* child to be born retarded."

"Or blind? Or deaf? Or with club feet?"

Marge's embarrassment grew. "Are you going to remind me of Helen Keller or Beethoven?"

"No," Betty Jo replied. "*You* reminded yourself of them."

"But their minds were fine."

"You mean their brains were not imperfect, don't you?"

"Yes. I'm confusing brain with mind."

Betty Jo's eyes remained patient. "The mind is eternal. It's the *thinking process* of the soul. It, being a part of the soul, is a part of God. God *is* perfect. Therefore, any part of God that is shared is a part of God's perfect-perfection. The soul is light, as is God. It's this light that I see in my son's eyes. Because my son's light is not distilled through the brain, his light shines more clearly. I see this every time I look deeply into his eyes or kiss his sweet face."

As Marge listened attentively, fear still stirred inside—a fear she dared not verbalize lest it have substance.

"Did you know that many blind people can see children?"

"No."

"Yes. Children, by the innocence of their nature, possess an aura so powerful that it's visible to the spiritual eye of the blind." Betty Jo paused. "The blind often can see the mentally retarded as well."

Despite Betty Jo having a retarded son, Marge kept wondering *why* Betty Jo was stressing this fact? "Is that because the mentally retarded forever retain the innocence of a child?"

"Yes. My son's imperfect brain has set his *perfect* mind free from corruption. There's eternal innocence in him. Even as he lives the human experience, he's showing us his spiritual nature. Those who turn away because of his physical nature tragically miss his true essence—his spiritual nature. If they'd pause to look, they would know that his presence gives them a glimpse of the greater *Him*. If they would only pause to look into his eyes, they'd see eternity. Sadly, they've avoided the rose because of its thorns."

Her battered emotions regrouping, Marge recalled the times she had turned away from a retarded child, not out of disgust but out of embarrassment. Her inability to react positively, no matter how innocent her intentions, became an act of rejection. That was what *turning away* equated to.

"Birth is when the breath begins and the mind is imprisoned," Betty Jo continued. "Ironically, death is when the breath stops and the mind is set free. Through death, one is truly born again."

The last thing Marge wanted to hear was anything connected with the word *death*. After all, she had just brought new life to the world.

"Mrs. Glider?"

Marge turned to the door. An older nurse entered the room to tell her about Barry.

"How is my baby?" Marge asked hesitantly.

"He's doing fine, dear. His legs are in full casts. Only his toes are showing. You'll be able to bring him home tomorrow. The doctor will change his casts weekly."

"Is this painful for Barry?"

"No," she replied. "He doesn't know any different."

"When can I see him?"

"I'll be bringing him in for his feeding shortly." Walking in brisk steps, the nurse turned and left the room.

Only afterward did Marge realize that the nurse had said nothing to Betty Jo, not even a slight greeting, not even a nod of the head.

Denny placed a dime in the coffee machine that sat in the hospital corridor. He took a few sips, then—chastising himself for buying machine coffee—tossed it in a container. In a few minutes, he would be taking Marge and Barry to his parents' house. Soon after, they would be living in their own home. From its foundation, he had studied his house with the same meticulous scrutiny that he studied life. From the wiring to the insulation to the wallboards, everything had its place—everything had to be perfect. From the moment of their storybook beginning—their meeting, engagement, wedding, Army, the house, and now their baby—he, like Marge, had written all scripts to have a happy ending: their first child would be a son, their second a daughter. After a day at the office, he would come home to a peaceful home nestled within the aroma of Italian pasta sauce and homemade cookies; he'd wrestle with his son, take him to ballgames, maybe even coach little league on a team where Barry would be a star.

He'd not brag about this, of course.

When his son was older, they'd attend Miami Hurricanes games dressed in matching green jerseys. They'd boo and cheer together. Before long he'd send Barry off to college, but not before one of those father-son talks. He had considered himself a very lucky man. Now he faced the possibility that the script he had penned might have its own ending.

A slight smile cornered his mouth as he recalled how he had teased Marge about *her* leanings toward romanticism versus reality, a trait she gladly admitted having. "Cinderella was always my favorite story. When I was a child, I'd dress up and pretend I was going to some wonderful ball where I'd meet my prince and live happily after all."

"Life isn't always a fairy tale," he had reminded.

"Why isn't it? Why *shouldn't* life have a happy ending?"

Maybe Marge was right. After all, what was wrong with viewing life as deserving of a happy ending? Wasn't that what everyone wanted, expected? As for Barry's legs, with casts, corrective shoes, and therapy, their son could be all he was meant to be. And even if the worst occurred—that Barry couldn't play football—so what?

So what?

Marge was dressed and waiting for Denny when the nurse brought Barry to them. The casts that claimed Barry's small legs made dressing him awkward. As Marge placed one of Barry's small arms in the sleeve of his baby gown, she felt her shoulders straighten with purpose and rebellion. "You'll walk and run, just like any other child," she promised. As though hearing her, Barry opened his eyes, already wide and blue, and she thought of how beautiful he was. "You're an angel," she whispered. "For a little while, just *for a little while*, one of your wings is broken."

As Barry studied her face, she wondered *why* she had been so afraid. He was absolutely wonderful, so amazingly beautiful that tears filled her eyes. Like a schoolgirl who finds herself embarrassed by a show of emotions, she hurriedly blinked back the tears. Holding Barry close, she nestled his neck, thinking that babies came to earth carrying the scent of God's breath. "Hi, Barry," she said softly. "I'm your mommy." Her face remained mesmerized for a moment longer. Smiling, she turned to Betty Jo. "Would you like to hold him?"

Betty Jo's eyes remained quiet, then, nodding, she held out her arms.

Marge gently placed Barry in this unusual woman's hold. Betty Jo laughed warmly. "He's so beautiful, Marge, so amazingly pure."

Marge looked at her gratefully. "You've been such a comfort to me. I was so frightened but you put things in perspective."

Holding Barry with a naturalness that no doubt came from having four children, Betty Jo's thin, almost curveless body filled with what appeared "light." Bowing slightly in reverence, Betty Jo handed Barry back to Marge. "I have a gift for you," she said warmly.

Cradling Barry, Marge tilted her head in question. She could not imagine what this gift could be since, while together, Betty Jo had never left the room nor had any outside contacts.

"Give me your right hand," Betty Jo said with simplicity. Extending her hand, Marge raised an eyebrow.

Betty Jo pressed a silver dollar in Marge's palm. "Place this in Barry's baby book. You and Denny are starting a new life. You'll do fine as long as you remember to live life by the motto on this coin."

Marge stared at the coin. As she turned the silver dollar over in her hand, she could feel Betty Jo's warmth on the coin. It spoke as Betty Jo had spoken—protectively, wisely. Every word Betty Jo had shared now appeared to have been born of a higher language, a gift from another world. Yet in truth, Betty Jo's gift to her was from this world, and it read: In God We Trust.

*****

A mother's memory of her five-year-old son

"Mommy, guess what I finded out today?"

"What, Barry?"

"I finded out that whirlin' 'round in circles to get dizzy takes lots a practice."

5

Friends

Life is a mystery to be lived, not a problem to be solved.

—Author Unknown

Even though Betty Jo was older than Marge, and even though it seemed apparent they came from different backgrounds, Marge felt that even apart, they were friends. Making no demands beyond her soft presence in the shared hospital room, Betty Jo had been able to reduce her pain. Once home with Barry, Marge attempted to recapture the sound of Betty's rich voice as well as trying to decipher *what* was said versus what was heard.

She hoped that the noise of her daily life would not drown out the truths offered by Betty Jo, or that her mind was not too full of the mundane to focus on these truths. Unfortunately, much of what Betty Jo had said had not yet settled into full understanding. There were little questions that her mind kept secret—questions born from thoughts she and Betty Jo had shared and questions that would replay in her mind as she went about her daily business.

Marge smiled as she looked down at Barry as he took his afternoon nap. Lying on his back in the crib with his casted legs off-center, she wondered how he could sleep with so much comfort? Denny came into the bedroom and stood beside her, then reached down for her hand, holding it gently. "The doctor said his casts could be off by Christmas."

Marge smiled.

"All in all, we're lucky," Denny added. "Lots of babies are born far worse. At least Barry's problems are fixable and temporary."

As though from some distant shore, drums of warning sounded. Marge experienced a repeat of an earlier sickening fear, one that suggested a certain battle in life had already been lost. Pressing her lips together, she deliberately denied what was happening and instead drew close to Denny, as though his presence would erase whatever uneasiness gripped her. "Barry's so beautiful, Denny. I love watching him sleep."

Barry awoke. He searched the room, then his blue eyes fixed upon Marge's face. He seemed as fascinated with her as she was with him. At the sight of Barry's awakening, Marge grew stronger and calmer. Her eyes locked with Denny's, and for the first time since Barry's birth, a feeling of oneness passed between them.

"Denny?" she asked. "Would it be possible for us to go for a drive this afternoon?"

Denny responded with an understanding smile. "Stir crazy already?" he asked.

"No," she replied. "I'd like to see how our house is coming along. Afterward, could we drive over to where Betty Jo lives? Before I left the hospital, I asked her for her address and phone number. I tried calling her to thank her for Barry's gift, but the operator said there was no such number."

"Maybe you copied it wrong."

"I must have. She's not listed in the book, but the address she gave me isn't out of our way. If she's not home, I'll leave a note in her mailbox with our phone number. I really need to keep in touch with her."

Denny stared at her in puzzlement. "*Need* to?"

"Yes. For some reason, I do."

Without argument, Denny agreed, then he reached down for Barry. He talked animatedly to him for a few minutes before laying him on the bed so that Marge could get him ready to go. Marge's hands were patient as she manipulated diapers with casts. "He's so small for these big things," she said. "Plus he can't wear most of those cute baby outfits people have given him."

It had been raining all morning, and now its moistness filled the afternoon air. The roads still held a smooth wet surface to them, while the surrounding scenery was more subdued, as though clouded by a slight mist. Despite the weather, Marge was enjoying the drive. The solitude of being alone with Denny and their son was welcomed, making the pending move into their own home that much more appreciated. Denny's parents were wonderful in opening their home to them, but two families together for any extent of time was one family too many.

As she settled back against the soft upholstery of the 1962 Ford her father had given her when she graduated from college, she again counted her blessings. She glanced up at the gray-blue sky and thought that even though she could not see the stars, they were still there, or as Betty Jo earlier reminded, "Remember, Marge, stars are often the brightest when it's the darkest."

Marge grew more anxious with each passing moment. When they reached the street where Betty Jo lived, she examined the piece of paper in her hand, careful not to jostle Barry. "It should be right here."

Denny drew their car to a stop. His eyes scrutinized the area. "Are you certain this is the address Betty Jo gave you?" he asked.

Marge nodded curiously as she glanced around. "It *has* to be here."

"Well," Denny replied, "It can't be."

"Why?"

"Look around. This is an empty lot." It was indeed just an overgrown weed-filled empty lot. There had never been a house there!

Marge's puzzlement was temporarily short-lived. The next day, November 22, 1963, President John F. Kennedy was assassinated in Dallas, Texas. Strained and desperately needing time alone with their new baby, they had earlier made reservations for the weekend at a Miami Beach hotel.

"This is so sad," Marge said quietly. "President Kennedy never had the chance to see his dreams completed."

Denny, despite not having voted for Kennedy, felt his throat tighten. Once again, he thought of Hal. "Kennedy never finished living out his natural life. That in itself is a tragedy. It goes against the order of things." Denny remembered how anxious he was to make a good living so that Marge and Barry could have everything possible, but he also was reminded of the truth that having money was not all there was to life. Once again, he knew that values had to be scrutinized. "John Kennedy will never have a chance to see his son grow or play football with him or just talk together," he added softly. Pausing, he thought how relative life was. "The Kennedys seemed to have it all—glamour, wealth, education, opportunity." His expression turned inward and became pensive.

Marge also grew pensive. Another sounding of fear pounded inside her—a sound that of late came to light when silence took hold.

Denny walked to a corner of their temporary bedroom where Barry slept. Marge hesitated, then followed. Together they looked down at their sleeping baby. The afternoon sun had created a golden halo around Barry's silken hair, and despite being large at birth, he appeared so very small and so totally helpless. He had the look of an angel, clean and innocent, with a sweetly smiling mouth and pink cheeks. Marge put her hand on Denny's arm and whispered, "Barry has the most tranquil face I've ever seen."

"I feel so bad that President Kennedy's son will never have the chance to grow up with his father. They won't be able to do those little things that build memories," Denny said almost inaudibly. "Yet at the same time, I feel so lucky that Barry and I will have a life together."

"I know. It's so sad, so terribly unfair." As her eyes swelled with compassion, Marge silently asked God to forgive her selfishness. She and Denny were so lucky, so wonderfully lucky. They might not have the trappings of people like the Kennedys, but they were alive. And so was Barry.

Their fairy-tale life was still in place. In the final analysis, all was well in their Camelot.

As it turned out, Barry only had to wear the casts for a little over a month. By Christmas, Marge was able to dress him in little red-and-white Santa pajamas. Barry's worst foot was put in a special corrective shoe that when worn turned the foot so that the shoe appeared to be on the wrong foot. Since he only had the one special shoe, people often told Marge that her baby had lost its "twin."

When Barry was three months old, their new home in Miramar was ready. Although twenty miles from Denny's parents, Denny's younger sister, Kay, and her husband, Sonny, resided nearby. Kay's daughter, Lori, was three; and their son, Lanny, was only six weeks older than Barry. "I'm so glad I have you around," Marge told Kay. "With Denny's new job in food sales requiring him to travel, I don't know what I'd do without you."

Marge took pride in showing off her home to Kay. The casement windows of their new home were opened to the air, allowing the fresh scent of the outdoors into the room. Shaking her head with a combination of awe and affection, Marge realized how much she loved their new home. She especially loved the entranceway atrium with its terrazzo floors—small pieces of marble embedded in polished mortar—a beautiful waterfall, and a small pond. Lush foliage and various-sized rocks gave the area an outdoor feeling. What was even more wonderful was that the dining room became part of the atrium when the inverted sliding glass doors were opened. Even during the most inclement weather, the sounds of nature—the waterfall, the pond, the plants—could be enjoyed.

The entire house hosted the same mosaic terrazzo floors, with the large sunken living room opening out onto a screened-in porch. The master bedroom, with its own bath and huge mirrored closet doors, led to the porch as did their garden kitchen and family room. With so much glass, the house was light and airy. Surrounding the porch was a fenced backyard with thick grass watered by an underground sprinkler system. In the far-left corner of the yard sat a swing set and a sandbox. As soon as financially possible, they planned to add shrubbery and flowering plants, although the developer had given them one small palm tree for their front yard, a tree they introduced as being part of the family.

At the front of the house, Barry's bedroom was separated from the spare bedroom by a full bath. It was a bedroom that would eventually belong to their next child who would be three years younger than Barry. As with Barry, Marge *knew* their second child would be a girl. Her name would be Sherry to rhyme with Barry.

After all, a son first and a daughter to follow was the planned Second Act of whatever fairy tale she continued to spin. Their first decorating extravagance were custom-made drapes of bright floral colors. A king-size bedroom set that was less than six months old had been purchased secondhand from one of Denny's fraternity brothers. Shortly after moving into their new home, a second extravagance occurred—the purchase of a color television set. "I can't wait for Barry to get old enough to watch football games with me," Denny expressed with the excitement of a young boy.

The rest of their furniture was either hand-me-downs or inexpensive imitations of what would come later. Once again, Marge thought of Betty Jo, perhaps because Betty Jo appeared worn but not worn out. Her "wornness" was more of a masterpiece rather than a cheap imitation. As suddenly as Betty Jo's face appeared, it disappeared, but not before Marge quietly asked, *Who are you? Where are you? And where did you come from?*

Shaking away the memory, Marge continued pointing out her treasures and non-treasures to Kay. Discussing Betty Jo was very difficult, plus she wasn't sure *how* to describe this strange woman to anyone. "Anyway," Marge added in reference to having secondhand furniture, "with Barry being little and into things, we won't have to worry about him messing up anything. Children are only babies for such a short while. Plus with you and Sonny living close and bringing Lori and Lanny over to play, the last thing we need are offlimit areas. We can make an investment in quality furniture when Barry's older, when he won't damage anything."

Hypnotized by her son, and pleased with having Kay's constant company, Marge watched Barry as he played on a mat on the living room floor. Kay's small son faced Barry on an adjoining mat, their only separation red, yellow, and blue rubber blocks. Nearby was an assortment of plastic trucks to push and to crash. Over a year old,

Barry was at the walking-tripping stage. Lanny, having a six weeks edge, was Barry's mentor and his challenge. She hoped Barry would soon imitate Lanny's grasp of language as well. Of course, she realized that vocabulary did not always arrive at the same developmental stage for each child. Worrying, of course, was silly.

"So," Kay asked, "has it been hard getting used to Denny's traveling?"

"Actually it's been kind of a relief," Marge explained. "That other job was driving him crazy, which was driving me crazy. Traveling gives Denny the kind of motion that makes him feel he's *going* somewhere."

Kay laughed. "If anyone will go somewhere, it's Denny. I know my brother. If there's a path to be found, he'll find it."

"And if he doesn't find a path, he'll make one," Marge added.

Suddenly her cheerfulness subsided. "The problem is not when he's traveling, but when he's home."

Kay's eyes widened with curiosity.

"When he's not out of town he's at a DeMolay meeting. Somewhere along the way, he was appointed governor of south Florida, so his duties have increased. Sometimes I feel that DeMolay is more important than we are."

"What do you mean?"

Almost as soon as she said it, Marge became annoyed with herself for having made such an observation. Her face held a faint flush to it as she tried to pull back, but then she decided that it might be too stressful *not* to continue on. Plus, Kay's warmth and her ability to listen often became a sedative. Slowly and reluctantly, she told Kay that Denny was leaving all the responsibilities of raising Barry to her. "I used to be a *real* person, an equal, not simply someone's wife and someone else's mother. I need a break now and then, especially with Barry and his constant earaches, high fevers, and the running back and forth to the doctor."

For a second, the conversation became forced as Kay remarked that Barry seemed to be getting *too* many fevers and earaches.

"I thought so too," Marge replied. "But the doctor thinks I'm chasing straws in the wind. Everyone thinks it's something

Barry'll outgrow. The doctor even suggested that if I had seven children, perhaps I wouldn't notice Barry so much. I was NOT making up his many ear infections and high fevers. I WAS OUT-RAGED!" Marge sighed, then returned to what she considered the real problem—Denny's lack of family involvement. "I know that parenthood isn't a spectator sport, but sometimes by the end of the day, I'm not sure I'm *not* just a spectator—one who's sitting on the sidelines watching life pass by. It's getting to the point I can't take it anymore."

"So don't take it."

Marge stood and walked toward the porch area, almost as though she wanted to pull as far away as possible from her complaints. The last thing she wanted was to appear as a possessive, whining wife, especially to Denny's sister whom she loved and admired. Without turning, she told Kay about another time when she couldn't take it and she had left. "It was when Denny was in the service. I was teaching high school across the street from Fort Lewis, and it was toward the end of the school year. I was about six months pregnant with Barry. Denny wanted to have his battalion over for a cookout that weekend. I said fine, but it had to be the following weekend because I had to grade finals. But you know Denny. He insisted it be the week-end of *his* choice. We really butted heads. I exploded and walked out. Of course, since we were living thousands of miles from home, this 'I can't take it anymore escape' was short-lived."

Kay handed Barry a truck to play with. With her face full of understanding, she looked at Marge. "And?"

Marge took in a deep breath, smiling slightly. "Well, I waited until nighttime. Being alone in a darkened park and having no place to go, I went home. Denny was so relieved to see me that he apologized and said he'd help me with everything—grade the papers, scrub floors, you name it."

"But you still ended up giving in, right?"

Although not liking the idea of history repeating itself, Marge lowered her eyes and nodded.

Kay stood. Her lovely red hair fell to her shoulders in a mass of color, and although her blue eyes were filled with understanding, they were also filled with humor. "Men!" she exclaimed.

"Yours too?" Marge asked as she glanced in the direction of Kay and the boys.

Kay's voice, rich with laughter, injected light into every inch of the room. "Men sometimes don't think, period. I read somewhere that all husbands are alike. The reason they have different faces is so you can tell them apart."

*****

A mother's memory of her five-year-old son

"MOMMY, GUESS WHAT I FINDED OUT TODAY?"
"What, Barry?"
"I FINDED OUT THAT DOGS DON'T LIKE PEAS."

6

Encounters

The harshest winter finds an invincible summer in us.

—Albert Camus

"Have you had Barry's hearing checked?" Denny's aunt asked delicately. She and Denny's uncle were visiting from Chicago for the Christmas holidays. They were anxious to see one-year-old Barry and to enjoy the warm Florida weather. "He doesn't seem to respond to sound."

The question was an unexpected shock to Marge. Ever since Barry had been a baby, he had been plagued with ear infections. From what she was told by the medical community, this was not unusual, and thus she was certain nothing was wrong with Barry's hearing. She shifted uneasily in her chair as they sipped tea in the sun-laden kitchen. "Barry's just stubborn," Marge responded. "He can hear fine if he chooses to."

"He acts as if he's in his own little world," Denny's aunt replied with her usual tranquility.

With a mixture of defense and anxiety, Marge turned to look at Barry as he sat playing with his toys. How could someone who was a stranger to Barry ask such a question? The truth was that from the time Barry was six months old, a gnawing fear had been preying on her mind. It was a fear she had deliberately pushed aside, as if to permit its examination would in itself cause the unthinkable: *Barry might be deaf!*

"He's just being a boy," Marge continued to say in defense of Barry. "You know how boys are, stubborn, doing what they want when they want."

A few moments of silence passed. Then despite her defensiveness and discomfort, Marge, in a tone that was *too* casual, asked Denny's aunt, "What makes you think something could be wrong with Barry's hearing?"

"We have some friends who have a deaf child, Marge," Denny's aunt said sadly. "Barry acts like that child."

Still grasping for whatever lifeline possible, Marge explained that perhaps Barry's problems centered around the pressure of new teeth coming in. "I had the dentist check him, and he didn't seem concerned. In fact, he seemed amused and said, I can pull teeth, but 'I can't make them grow.'" Suddenly remembering something, Marge smiled. "It's funny. I could have sworn Barry had been born with teeth. When I tried to nurse him, it took several tries for him to catch on. He learned with so much gusto I swore he'd bitten me."

Marge paused as she once again looked at Barry. From the moment of his birth, he had continued to grow and gain weight at a normal rate. She had noted his first real smile when he was five weeks old; at six weeks, his baby talk had begun. By the time he was two months, he was rolling over from his tummy to his back and two months later from his back to his tummy, which made him laugh out loud. At that time, he was also scooting and pushing back in his walker. At five months, he was crawling, which he did by pulling his body forward with his arms, his legs going in every direction. By seven months, he was crawling *and* pulling himself up on furniture. It was while he was still five months old that they had taken him to a restaurant and he had looked at Denny and shouted "Da-Da"—a feat he was so proud of that he continued to shout it from his high chair the entire night. Denny, of course, was equally proud that an obvious male bonding had begun.

In truth, Barry was an exceptionally intelligent child who in many ways was ahead of other children, something that Marge—not wanting to appear as a bragging mother—*only* pointed out to Denny, to Kay, to her parents, to Denny's parents. And a few others.

Everyone got a kick out of how at eight months Barry would throw out his chest, pull in his chin and shoulders, and grin like a little general. By his first birthday, despite heavy corrective shoes, he simply "let go" and walked across the patio as though he had been secretly practicing. He was as active and as smart as any toddler. He was also very mischievous. During his first birthday party, he brought his little hand down in the middle of the cake, palm open, and laughed with delight as he smeared it, and the ice cream, all over his face. While the ten children invited to his party played with his new toys, Barry chose to play with boxes. His imagination was obvious as one box became a train and another a truck. It was at his birthday party that Marge had discovered his first tooth, top and front.

Pushing the memory aside, she looked at Denny's aunt and restated, "Although some teeth have come in, maybe those teeth that haven't broken through are causing some pressure. That's possible, isn't it?"

Denny's aunt tilted her head with some surprise at Marge's analysis. "Perhaps," she said with discomfort. "I mean, let's hope that's all it is."

Seeming to sense he was the focus of their conversation, Barry smiled at them charmingly. As he pulled himself up and walked over to her, Marge watched him with a certain entrancement. Looking at him, she felt encouraged.

Her breath came easier. There was absolutely *nothing* wrong with Barry's hearing. He was simply an inquisitive, stubborn little boy who deliberately *chose* to be in his own world from time to time. That's all there was to it.

As she picked up Barry in order to allow him to have a sip of her tea, she deliberately avoided the concern still evident on Denny's aunt's face. Instead, she proudly displayed Barry's ability to manipulate a cup. The tension was broken when Barry stuck all ten of his fingers into the liquid.

Later that night, she was awakened by a dream of Betty Jo. She wasn't sure if Betty Jo had said these words in the hospital or if it had been part of her dream. "*You can't always alter the course that life takes. You can only alter what you expect from it. Forget things as they once were. Accept them as they now are.*"

If Denny was concerned over Barry, he tried not to show it, although at times he wondered about a certain frenziness in Barry's movements. Never having a child before, he told himself he really had no idea what "normal" was. Standing on the back patio, he noted that although the dark, clear sky was burning bright with the full light of stars, the night air was close. Dwelling on any concerns over Barry had been lessened by traveling. When home, he couldn't help recognize how intelligent Barry appeared and how he loved playing with his toys, *especially* those that made noise. Of course, there was that time when he and Marge had taken eight-month-old Barry to Atlanta. Prior to Atlanta, Barry had been the perfect traveler. This particular time, Barry would not allow Marge nor Denny to put him down without throwing a tantrum. He cried all night. Even after arriving home, he would wake in the middle of the night, terrified.

They had convinced themselves that being away from familiar surroundings had frightened him and that he'd soon readjust, which he did. Still, Denny wondered if that was a sign of *something* wrong? Had Barry been suffering some sort of overlooked physical pain?

As for a hearing problem, the only time Barry didn't respond was when he was involved in playing. To admit that Barry only responded when he was looking directly at them was to admit that his aunt might be right—*that something was wrong with Barry.*

There wasn't. There couldn't be. The club foot situation had been taken care of. The worst was behind them. He was simply overreacting to traveling on the road and a busy schedule. Without knowing exactly why, he felt the need to take a walk.

Marge's self-denial did not last much longer. Even during the drive with Denny to the audiologists, she continued to convince herself that it was Barry's personality that kept him in his own little world. "I'm afraid, Denny," she finally admitted.

Giving her a brave smile, he nodded then said, "Let's not jump to conclusions."

"It could be his developing teeth, some sort of pressure."

"Maybe."

She reminded herself that they had made the appointment to prove Denny's aunt wrong. After all, no one else had said anything about Barry's hearing. Besides, how could Barry respond to them so effectively and be so bright if something was wrong with his hearing? True, she had begun to sneak up on him and clap her hands. Sometimes there had been response.

Sometimes there had been none.

"What if it's true?" she asked. "What *if* something is wrong with Barry's hearing?" She could not say the word *deaf*.

"If something's wrong, then we'll handle it."

Marge sighed heavily. She could not imagine what her little boy's future would be like *if* he were deaf. What would it be like to live in the sound of silence? She shook her head to rid herself of that awful word. Deafness was a problem that other people faced, not them. Again she shook her head, this time to rid herself of such a selfish thought regarding *other people*.

They simply were *not* "other people."

As they sat in the reception room waiting for the doctor to complete his tests, Marge was so flushed that nothing could cool her. In order to fill the wait, she picked up a magazine and, as was a habit, began leafing through it from back to front. Suddenly she paused and turned back a few pages. The word *angels* had caught her eye. She began to read:

> By nature, angels are beings of pure eternal spirit, a different race of beings from humans in that they are messengers of God sent to earth. Their stay may be brief, but their journey is everlasting. They often watch over people, guide them, and save them from disasters. In the end, they leave earth a better place than they found it. They are God's celestial bridge between the spiritual and the physical. They speak from the heart to the heart.

Betty Jo's face flashed in her mind, but before she had time to explore this memory, the doctor called them to his office. The results of Barry's hearing test had come in: he only had 20 percent hearing in one ear and 40 percent in the other.

A thick, heavy silence filled the room as Marge contemplated the doctor's words. Shocked, she kept looking at Denny, begging him to give her hope. There was none. She looked back at the doctor. "I don't understand," she protested. "With so little hearing, *how* does Barry respond to us, talk to us?"

"Barry's extremely smart," the doctor said. "He can actually read lips, which is amazing in a child so young. Remember, Barry is not totally deaf." Knowing the devastation inflicted, the doctor explained he was going to fit Barry with a hearing aid in his best ear. "This will help somewhat. Also, it would be best if you enroll Barry in speech therapy."

"I can't believe this," Marge said weakly. Her normally tanned face grew pale, and her muscles grew tight. Unconsciously, she pulled back as far as possible from the doctor. Stunned, she looked at Denny. He, too, was shaking with disbelief. She felt as if she had been hit with a one-two punch—first the club feet and the possibility that he might never walk, now this!

"Barry can live a normal life," the doctor stressed. "His speech should be on par by the time he goes into the second grade. He's very intelligent. Remember, it's *only* his hearing that's affected. He's completely normal in all other areas. I have no doubt that by the time Barry is ready for the second grade, he'll be caught up enough for regular school. Before then, perhaps when Barry's around five, I suggest you send him to the Florida State School for the Deaf in Northern Florida. In the meantime, let's consider speech therapy."

And Marge thought, *I will never send my baby away!*

"We'll take whatever steps are necessary," Denny promised, his voice strong and determined. Turning, he reached over and wiped a tear from Marge's face. "Barry'll be fine, Marge. He has a wonderful mind, quick and alert. Think about that. Think about how fast he catches on. After speech therapy, he'll sail through life."

A wave of sickness passed through Marge. "Barry's only a baby," she murmured. She turned to the doctor. "Are you certain there's no mistake?"

"Have as many examinations as you want," the doctor replied with sympathetic understanding. "The results will be the same."

Marge's head fell to her chest in incredulous despair.

The doctor took her visibly shaking hands in his. "Mrs. Glider, everything will turn out all right. Remember what I just told you: Barry is very intelligent. It's *only* his hearing that's affected."

*****

A mother's memory of her five-year-old son

"Mommy, guess what I finded out today?"
"What, Barry?"
"I finded out that clams don't make good pets."

7

Another Autumn

When the outlook is poor, try the uplook.

—Author Unknown

Marge was the first to see the arc of colors after the brief rain shower. She recalled that someone had told her it took both the sun and the rain to make a rainbow.

Had that *someone* been Betty Jo? So much time had passed that Betty Jo seemed more a mirage than a reality. It had reached the point where she was no longer sure of whether words spoken by Betty Jo were the result of recent dreams or a result of their time together. It all ran together. Turning, she watched Barry chase his dog, Misty, around the backyard. Although his vocabulary was still limited, his squeals of delight said it all. Since he was a toddler, his loss of hearing was not noticeable to strangers. Despite the medical community's assurance that Barry would eventually be like other boys his age, in the privacy of her mind, she feared this loss of hearing could isolate him.

Like most parents, she wanted her son's life to be as flaw-free as possible. As it had turned out, Barry's first year of life had been anything but that. She tried praying, but her prayers were colored in doubt. Some spiritual strength had disappeared or perhaps had never been there to begin with. On another level, she felt helpless in seeking strength from a power she was beginning to think had deserted her. She also felt that in some way, her lack of faith might be limiting God's powers, or that with faith, she would be granted rewards. She knew such reasoning held its own blindfolds and was arrogant. She truly wanted to *understand* and thus accept events with trust, but *wanting* to believe and *believing* stood diversely apart. Thus, no matter how hard she tried, she repeatedly asked God, "*Why are You allowing this to happen?*"

She only hoped that fear was a part of some necessary experience that would ultimately bring her to total faith. Once again, the image of Betty Jo filled her mind and with it came the words, *There is silence in the dark cocoon before the butterfly emerges. Then there is music, and there is light. What is often invisible to the eye is seen with the soul. Be in tune with yourself.*

She blinked and the image was gone.

When she told her mother and father about the doctor's diagnosis of Barry, her parents, whose entire world revolved around their only grandchild, insisted they see another doctor. Sadly, after more extensive testing, a second confirmation was given with added words, "You're fortunate to live near two of the best hearing centers in the state, the University of Florida and the University of Miami."

Barry would be two in a few months and had been fitted for his first hearing aid, a mold that was attached to a long cord. Because the cord was attached to a battery and battery unit, it was necessary to buy Barry shirts with pockets. He was very good about wearing his mold *unless* he decided to feed it to his dog, Misty.

Barry walked to her and said, "Mama, hot!"

Despite an earlier shower, the summer heat was sweltering. With its steamy pungency came the smell of wet grass and wilting flowers. The day's heaviness made it too hot to take Barry to the beach. In the distance, she heard the sound of heat thunder. Perhaps another shower would make the day more durable.

"Mama, hot!" Barry repeated, knowing no other words to explain his discomfort. His limited vocabulary consisted of words such as: *Mama, Daddy, bye-bye, hot, dog,* and *boat.*

Marge studied Barry to see if his hand touched either ear, a sign of an earache. This time the word *hot* meant *hot*. "Let's go inside where it's cool," Marge said. Before turning to open the door to the kitchen, she saw the empty cord dangling from Barry's pocket. "Barry!" she cried in panic. "Did you feed Misty your ear mold again?"

Barry smiled widely and proudly.

"Oh, Barry! Those molds cost twenty-five dollars apiece! We don't have the money to keep replacing them. You can't keep feeding them to Misty!"

As she crawled on her hands and knees across the grass searching for the ear mold, Barry happily joined in the search, crawling beside her. Every time he found something, he squealed, then handed her stones, bugs, and small pieces of sticks. He even handed her the decaying remains of one of Misty's dog bones. Misty, in the meantime, thought the search was a game of pick-up-sticks and grab-the-bone-and-run.

No ear mold was found.

Exhausted and defeated, Marge wiped her soiled hands across her sweaty forehead, leaving behind dark streaks of dirt. Shaking her head futilely, it became clear another week of casseroles and hot dogs would be eaten.

When one reached the end of a rope, sometimes the only thing to do was tie a knot and hang on. "Well, Misty," Marge scolded, "somewhere in your hairy body rests Barry's ear mold, which is about as useful to you as a clock in an empty house."

With or without the added cost of dog-fed ear molds, their budget was tight. Orthopedic shoes, Barry's hearing problems, and the twice-a-week seventy-mile round trips for speech therapy classes continually drained them. She was thankful her parents lived nearby. When their diet of hamburger, hot dogs, and chicken ran the gamut, her parents treated them to a nice dinner at a restaurant. When she invited them to her home, she splurged on the cheapest cut of roast possible which, no matter how long it marinated, usually arrived at the table tough and tasteless.

Luckily their social life consisted of other couples their age who also had to decorate their home in "early poverty." One couple they were particularly close to were Roy and Sandy Wilson. They often shared thrown-together dinners that were followed by a game of cards and discussion of children. One evening, Denny asked a coworker, Walt, and his wife, Carole, over to play bridge and meet the Wilsons. During the conversation, Carole casually mentioned she was a special education teacher of the deaf in Dade County. Marge felt as if a door had swung open, that Carole's presence was "meant to be." She immediately began a series of questions.

Carole's eyes shone as she explained the wonderful work being done. "These children are very special, Marge, and very intelligent. Sadly, though, there are too few schools for the deaf and hearing-impaired. This school offers top-notch education for children who otherwise have nowhere to turn."

Marge, puzzled about the lack of education for children with special needs, explained Barry's condition. "I didn't know there was help available so close to where we live. Would Barry be eligible?"

Carole's eyes dimmed. "There's a long waiting list. Plus, you live in Broward County rather than Dade County."

Marge felt her heart sink. She turned and looked at Sandy, who adored Barry and thought he was extremely bright. "What do you think I should do?"

Sandy hesitated, then reached across the table and covered Marge's hand with hers. "I'd suggest you go directly to the school board and petition them to admit Barry into their fall term. If you're refused, ask again and again."

Whether through timing, luck, or divine intervention, Barry was accepted into Dade County's program shortly before his third birthday. Going through the various channels had been difficult, but their persistence paid off. They had to obtain a letter from Broward County stating that no help of this kind was available. When Dade County granted permission for Barry's enrollment, it came with the stipulation that Marge or Denny would provide transportation.

Agreement was happily given. At this point, Marge would have agreed to drive Barry back and forth to Mars if asked!

Barry was allowed to attend classes for the deaf at Biscayne Gardens Elementary School in Miami. When Marge left the school building, the sun was shining so bright it startled her. Shielding her eyes, she looked around and thought this symbolized her own darkness opening to the light. Momentarily looking down, she caught sight of a wildflower groping its way through a crack in the brick walkway. It, in its reach for the sun, seemed to whisper, *I, too, have the right to go beyond the limits that try to confine me.*

There were times when Marge felt she was being led through life, while at other times she knew her steps were deliberate. When she discovered she was again pregnant, she was uncertain of her feelings. She and Denny had talked about having another child, even at times four children, with at least two years between each.

"We're two months ahead of schedule," she told Denny.

His amused voice reassured her. "It's one of the few things that's been ahead of schedule lately," he teased.

She smiled. "Considering Barry's problems, our budget and your traveling, maybe we should have planned this better."

"All of that can be worked out." He paused to ask, "Are you okay with this?"

"Yes." She wanted her smile to reassure him, as well as to reassure that she believed their second child would be healthy in every way. "I believe in family planning. Still, isn't it funny that everybody who's in favor of population control has already been born."

It was another beautiful day and another doctor's visit. A sense of restlessness caused her to remember Betty Jo and to once again question *who* she was. And *why* was it that whenever she sat in the doctor's waiting room, she kept stumbling over magazine articles about angels? It was happening again.

> By allowing angels into your life, you are actually tuning into your soul and a higher vibration—a pure light vibration composed of love, faith, and truth.

Marge shook her head, thinking, *Do I need an angel?*

As though an answer to her question, she heard Betty Jo say, *Our worries and fears about tomorrow lessen the powers we have over today. Today is the only day we have.*

Miscarriage both answered and solved a problem: there had been something wrong with this second pregnancy. The doctor told her that she was healthy and could have other children. "Nature often takes care of problems."

As she had done when carrying Barry, she returned to the ocean in order to think. It was impossible *not* to embrace another fear: would all their future children be born with physical problems? It was too horrid a fear to delve into. She was also afraid that to contemplate this fear would be to give it substance. To live in fear was to *unlive*. She thought about this revelation and wondered if it had come from her. Whatever it was, she had to reconnect with herself. As soon as this decision was made, she experienced a current of calm energy.

Looking out over the waters, she recalled the story of the oyster: It was a grain of sand that penetrated the oyster's shell to the point that the oyster, in order to relieve this irritation, coated the sand with a soothing balm. When the liquid hardened, a precious pearl was formed. From what appeared misery was created a jewel.

By the time Barry started school at Biscayne Gardens, she was full of hope and happiness. "Come on," she smiled bravely as she took Barry by the hand and led him to his class. "You're going to have so much fun! You're just like one of those big boys going to school. You'll learn to read and to write."

A week later, she was happily surprised when Barry decided he was too big to have a "mommy" walk him to class. "I go, Mommy. You stay in car."

Marge smiled as she reached across to open the door, but her heart was hammering in her throat as Barry eagerly jumped out of the car, then turned to wave at her. "Bye-bye, Mommy. I go to somewhere."

When she shared Barry's independence with Denny, he tilted his head. "And did you just drive away?

"Well, no, not exactly," she admitted.

"You followed him secretly to be sure he found his way, right?" She blushed. "Ummmm, sort of. I like to think of it as being Barry's guardian angel."

Denny laughed. "Aren't guardian angels supposed to be invisible?"

Marge looked at Denny directly. "I always thought so. Now I'm not so sure."

It was still early morning when Marge plugged in the Christmas tree lights. Her excitement grew at the thought of seeing Barry's face as he opened his presents from Santa. Although at first frightened of the "white-bearded one," Barry now loved the fat man so much that he would hold his tummy and say, "Ho-Ho-Ho."

Quickly removing signs that Santa had forgotten to consume the milk and cookies Barry left, she noted Barry had taken a few nibbles out of each of Santa's cookies. She laughed, turned on the radio for Christmas carols, then looked around to see if the atmosphere was ready for a little boy and his toys. Normally when she arose early, she took care to be quiet, but this morning, she deliberately made enough noise to waken everyone. Because Barry loved horses, especially the Shetland pony her brother owned, her parents had spent the night in order to see Barry's face when he saw his rocking horse, cowboy boots, fringed chaps, cowboy hat, shirt, and vest. Hanging over the saddle was a gun and holster set.

For weeks, the preparation for Christmas had been one of the most fun times of her life: the baking of sugar cookies cut in the shapes of trees, bells, candy canes, and Santa Clauses. Barry, between stuffing his mouth, helped spread the icing as well as to hang upon the tree ornaments he had made at school. "I made angel," he earlier said. "Put angel there." He pointed to a lower branch of the tree.

"Shouldn't I put the angel on the top of the tree?"

"No. Put 'er there so I can touch 'er."

Barry's paper-mache angel consisted of two vertical pieces of paper with a circle pasted on top for the head. The paper was positioned so that one vertical created a gown while the back vertical became angel wings. One of the wings was broken. "What happened here?" Marge asked. "Your little angel has a broken wing."

Barry tilted his head in deep thought. "It has a boo-boo. You fix it."

Fixing any boo-boo meant putting a Band-Aid over wounds, whether real or imaginary. Marge touched the angel with its broken wing, now *fixed* by a Band-Aid and thought it looked both silly and precious. The angel also represented Barry's improvement in speech. With only five children to a class, Barry was excelling so rapidly that few doubted his readiness for regular school when the time was right. Turning the Christmas music up, she walked over to where Barry's baby book sat and from it took the silver dollar, secured it with a piece of ribbon, and carefully placed it beside the winged angel. The motion of attaching the silver dollar to the tree made the coin turn and vibrate with light.

With its turning, the angel's wings fluttered slightly.

"Thank you, Betty Jo," she whispered.

Hearing the sounds of motion, she turned and smiled at Denny who was carrying a still-drowsy Barry. Tiptoeing behind were her parents.

"Mommy!" Barry squealed as he reached toward the lights. "Hot!" Seeing his horse, he almost jumped out of Denny's arms. "Horsey! Barry's horsey!"

As Barry rocked on his horse with the type of energy only a child has, Marge noticed a string running from the tree to the floor and finally to the garage. She looked at Denny in question.

"Follow it," he indicated.

As she followed the string, Denny and her parents followed her. Their adventure ended in the garage behind the trunk of Denny's car. Inside the trunk was a beautiful hand-carved wooden jewelry chest. "When did you do this?" she asked.

"I had nothing to do with it. Santa did it in the middle of the night."

Marge tilted her head. "Methinks Santa had a helper."

He laughed. "Think of it more as my being Santa's guardian angel."

"Santa doesn't have a guardian angel."

"I'm not sure. Maybe *everyone* has a guardian angel."

Marge paused as she thought back over the past few years. "I'm beginning to think this may be truer than imagined."

"This is a good day."

Watching her parents return inside the house, Marge turned to Denny. "It's a better day than you know. I have a surprise gift for you as well."

"It's not in the garage, is it?"

"Yes." Marge laughed at Denny's puzzlement. Then she patted her abdomen. "We're going to have a real angel. Next year, at this time, there will be gifts under the tree for Sherry."

Denny's expression changed to shock. "*Sherry?*"

"Barry's going to have a sister in September." Hugging Denny with confidence, Marge added, "I *know* this baby will be born and that everything will be fine. And I *know* it will be a girl."

When they returned to the house, they noted that Barry was playing with a gift box rather than a toy. Denny knelt. "That's a very nice box," he complimented.

"It's a train," Barry corrected.

"Next Christmas, Santa will bring someone else boxes too. You'll have a baby sister."

"Tister?" Barry repeated.

Denny nodded.

Picking up the box he was playing with, Barry walked over to Marge. "Here, Mommy," he said as he handed her his prized toy. "Put tister in this."

Marge's laughter proved how much she now trusted her right to be happy. She wanted to sing every Christmas carol ever written, especially those with the word *angel* in them. She wanted to sing out to the world that Sherry Leigh Glider would soon make her presence known.

She looked at the angel still swinging on the tree, Barry's broken-winged angel, and thought the worst was behind them.

All was well again.

*****

A mother's memory of her five-year-old son

"MOMMY, GUESS WHAT I FINDED OUT TODAY?"

"What, Barry?"

"I FINDED OUT THAT JESUS WAS BORN THE SAME DAY SANTA CLAUS COMES!"

8

Few Shadows

Autumn—the year's last, loveliest smile.

—William Jennings Bryant

Marge's "expansion" began to interrupt her promise to remain happy and grateful. "Driving Barry to and from school is becoming more difficult," she complained.

Denny was not listening. Having risen to governor of South Florida with the DeMolays, he was busy changing clothes for yet another meeting. When he wasn't traveling, he was out almost every night.

"I don't understand why you have to stop by and see your parents after the meetings. You never get home until eleven. Barry rarely sees you anymore. I never see you anymore."

He gave her an exasperated "don't nag me" look. "I'll concentrate on Barry this weekend. I promise."

Marge sat heavily in a bedroom chair, hoping that beyond practically raising Barry alone, her clumsiness would bring to his attention another baby was on the way. Rather than taking the bait, he bent down and placed a quick kiss on her forehead. "Didn't you say Kay was coming over to keep you company?" he asked as though the issue was not a missing husband/father but rather one of loneliness.

"Yes," Marge said sadly.

"Good," Denny replied with relief. Almost as an afterthought he added, "If you need me, you have numbers where I can be reached. I'm only a telephone call away."

Marge sat quietly for a moment more. As he raced from the bedroom and toward the front door, she whispered, "Yes, Denny, I have the telephone numbers where you can be reached. But there may come a point when I don't *want* to reach you."

*****

"You seem down in the dumps," Kay observed. "Is everything okay with Barry?"

"Barry's coming along fine," Marge answered angrily. "Thanks to me and the school, that is."

"Denny?" Kay asked, knowing her question was also the answer.

Marge grunted a reluctant yes. "He's always gone. I'm sick and tired of being both mother *and* father to Barry."

"Have you told him how you feel?"

Marge nodded. "All the time. In fact, I've become a nag. Not that he notices. He simply doesn't see me or listen to me. His mind is always someplace else."

"It's been said that the best marriages are between a deaf husband and a blind wife."

Marge scowled. "Denny may be deaf, but I'm not blind. Near-sighted perhaps but definitely not blind."

Kay looked at Marge, who despite being in the last stages of pregnancy, was still pretty. Yet also sad. "Sometimes men see only in the dimension they can manage."

"It's strange. When Denny and I first married, I saw our life as a fairy tale, with the first chapter written in poetry." Marge sighed with disenchantment. "Now it seems the rest of our chapters have been written in cheap prose."

"Being pregnant often makes you see things worse than they are," Kay suggested. "Hormones, backaches—the type of changes that occur while carrying new life."

"Kay, it's *not* my pregnancy that's the problem. I have no morning sickness, no real pains other than lots of swift kicks from Sherry." Despite her anger with Denny, Marge smiled. "I think Sherry's going to be a flamenco dancer." Looking at where Sherry rested, Marge added, "She's worth it. But I'm not sure Denny is. Sometimes I believe that when I married Denny, I not only quit my job but I quit my life."

Kay started to offer more advice but thought better of it.

Marge's tone turned deadly serious. "I've been thinking about leaving Denny."

Kay stared at Marge, aghast.

"I could move into my parent's home temporarily, at least until Sherry's born. After that, I could return to teaching."

Kay studied Marge for a moment, then looked at her watch. "I've got to run," she announced as she hurried out the front door.

Stunned, Marge shrugged her shoulders. Two hours later, Denny came slamming into the house. Marge showed surprise at his early arrival and anger on his face.

"What the hell have you told my parents?" he shouted.

Still stunned, Marge's eyes widened in surprise, followed by the revelation of *why* Kay had retreated so suddenly: Kay had told the Gliders that they had to speak with Denny. Marge learned later that they had sternly reprimanded their twenty-eight-year-old son: "Go home to your wife and child. Marge is pregnant, Barry has hearing problems. You don't belong here every night, you belong with them. That's your home now, and they're your family. If they don't become more important than your DeMolay meetings, then you will lose them. *Go home!*"

*****

"You're in the early stages of labor," the doctor told Marge during a routine appointment.

It was September 12, 1966. Although Sherry was due soon, she had no idea she was in labor. "Are you sure?" Marge asked. "I don't have any pains."

"You've begun to dilate," the doctor advised. "But you have plenty of time to go home and pack."

Because Barry's school and Denny's parents' home were close to the doctor, Marge decided to drive there in order to call Denny at work rather than chance the twenty-mile trip home alone. During the drive to the Gliders, she mentally listed what had to be done: Have Denny meet her at his parents', pick up Barry from school, have Denny follow her home, pack, drive to the hospital. Have Sherry.

Sherry! She was going to have Sherry! She knew it would happen, but *now* it was happening! She gave God a quick word of thanks. She also silently thanked the Gliders for coming to her defense two months earlier. Once Denny's embarrassed anger had subsided, he realized how close he had come to losing his family. Although not totally an "at-home husband and father," he had made significant strides toward becoming more conscious of his family.

Nervously pacing the Gliders' living room, Marge tripped over one of the colored blocks Barry had left behind during one of his visits. Since Barry had been so young when his hearing problem was discovered, he could not tell them about hearing sounds. In order to communicate, he was given colored blocks to drop into a coffee can when he heard a sound. Because he was extremely bright, it had not taken long to teach him how to respond properly. The audiologist, wearing earphones, had sat in a windowed control room in order to test Barry.

Barry thought the entire matter was a wonderful game.

This thought reminded Marge of Barry's second set of grandparents, her mother and father. Crazy about Barry, her parents visited several weekends a month. One Sunday afternoon, as they were preparing to leave, Barry said he wanted to go home with them.

"Not this time, honey," Marge had replied.

"Barry go bye-bye too," he responded, stomping out of the room.

A little while later, they walked into Barry's bedroom and found him packing his clothes in a paper bag. "And just what are you doing?" she asked.

"I go bye-bye to somewhere. Now."

Laughing at the memory, she thought she should telephone her parents, but the sound of Denny's car interrupted this idea. She'd call them later.

"Are you okay?" Denny asked nervously as he rushed in the house. "Are you sure we'll have time to pick up Barry at the school?"

"Slow down, Denny. I'm fine. We've plenty of time."

Not even Barry's teacher was convinced that time was on their side. They made it to the hospital by noon. "You still have some hours to go," she was told. "As with Barry's birth, we'll use sodium pentothal. I don't believe in mothers suffering during childbirth."

"Be careful what you say," Denny teased Marge. "Sodium pentothal's also a truth serum."

"No," Marge teased back, "*you* need to be careful of what I say."

Denny feigned shock, then gave her a gentle pat on the shoulder. "I'll take Barry to my parents' house, then I'll be right back."

Five hours later, Sherry Leigh Glider was born.

"Sherry was perfect, healthy, and beautiful." Marge blinked at how perfect her new daughter was. Through her tears, she saw Sherry's huge blue eyes and bright-red cheeks. Sherry was healthy in every way. "Thank you, God," she whispered. "And forgive my doubts and lack of faith."

"She looks like she's wearing rouge," Denny remarked as he sat on the edge of the hospital bed.

"Denny?" Marge asked. "Promise me you'll be around more for Sherry than you were for Barry. I can't raise two children by myself. And I don't want to raise them by myself."

Denny nodded. "I promise."

Although only in the hospital for one night, Marge again thought of Betty Jo and, with the memory, more words: *Joy and laughter cannot be purchased and can only be received or given as a gift. Joy lightens the darkest room and lessens the worst of fears. When you taste joy, hold it, and share it.*

Despite finding comfort in Betty Jo's words, despite reexperiencing her voice, an uneasiness lingered, one too difficult to define. Somewhere deep inside, she felt that Betty Jo had been *sent* into her life for a specific reason. What that reason was confused her, yet she knew that somehow, she was living in a state of *waiting*.

Because she had almost starved Barry by attempting to breast-feed, she decided Sherry would be bottle-fed. After Sherry was returned to the hospital nursery, Marge casually asked Denny, "Do you believe in angels?"

"Mmmm, yes. Sure, why not? They're written about in the Bible. Plus I read somewhere that angels congregate just below the clouds."

For a second, Marge's pulse quickened, almost as if she had stumbled by accident upon an explanation to Betty Jo's existence. Yet as she thought about this possibility, it became an impossibility. After all, Betty Jo didn't resemble what she perceived an angel to look like—thin, almost ragged in appearance, and seemingly impoverished.

She then thought of Jesus.

Denny was right. Many books in the Bible mentioned angels as servants of God. Angels had appeared to Abraham, Daniel, Ezekiel, John, and to Jesus's Mother, Mary. Angels were said to come to earth with missions. They appeared in many forms but mostly human form. In truth, she couldn't recall one story of an angel being garbed in gowns that shimmered or with hair that was golden or skin that was ethereal.

Those were "Cinderella" images, part of the fairy-tale myth she and others had conjured up in order to ease the hard edges of reality. Considering these thoughts caused a feeling of peace to come over her, and with it, she fell into a much-needed sleep. She only barely felt Denny's kiss on her forehead before he tiptoed out of her room, barely heard him say, "I'll see you in the morning, honey."

She was floating upward, almost as though she were a gentle breeze warmed by the rising sun. She had no wings, yet she was floating further into herself and outside herself. She saw colors no man could paint and scents no man could create. Within her floating, she saw images that became too hazy to grasp, yet they were comforting, almost pulsating. Thoughts required no effort, and her imagination was unlimited. She could smell tomatoes ripening in a garden, heard birds hunting seeds, even *heard* the rising of the sun. Memories were flying around her like the pink of an early morning, some forgotten until that moment. It seemed as if she were having a reunion with herself. She learned that more was accomplished by kindness and faith than by force and fear. As she floated, she was fed patience. Terror of the unknown was nonexistent. Something had freed her from the confines of her physical body, and for one golden moment, she had been granted a view of the spiritual and with it was able to sip the cool, geode waters of the eternal.

We are all born for a purpose. It is the same for everyone.

Marge was jolted from sleep. She looked at the bed next to her. It was empty. Or was it? Betty Jo had offered those same words, yet the words in her dream had not come from Betty Jo this time. They were not words spoken by a familiar voice, yet at the same time the voice was not unfamiliar.

Quietly absorbing the stretches of this strange experience, she questioned, "*Why* am I hearing these words *now* when everything is so perfect?"

*****

A mother's memory of her five-year-old son

"MOMMY, GUESS WHAT I FINDED OUT TODAY?"

"What, Barry?"

"I FINDED OUT THAT GOLDFISHES DON'T LIKE PEAS NO BETTER'N DOGS DO."

9

In the Shadows

Time is nature's way of preventing everything
from happening at once.

—Anonymous

Backgrounded by the sunlight that was streaming in through the
sliding glass doors, there was something mystical about Barry. As
his hands grabbed at the dust particles floating within the beams,
Marge's expression turned to rapture. Barry's feet barely touched the
floor as he leaped about, clutching at what appeared to be a swarm-
ing universe. Tilting her head, Marge asked, "What are you doing,
Barry?"

Barry continued grabbing at the late morning's golden rays. "I
catch the sun," he replied matter-of-factly.

Smiling, Marge continued with the preparation of his lunch,
happy that his communication skills had rapidly improved. Sherry,
nestled in a padded baby seat on the kitchen floor, awoke and began
to cry for lunch. Barry turned from his sun-catching dance in order
to strike an authoritative pose. "Tister hungry. I feed her."

"I'll tell you what, how about if when I change Tister's diapers
you powder her, okay?"

"Okay," Barry replied as he eagerly climbed upon a kitchen stool
to await Marge's placement of a towel on the counter upon which to

change Sherry. After removing Sherry's diapers, Marge handed Barry the powder. As he began powdering Sherry's round bottom, Marge looked away for a second. When she looked back Barry had powdered Sherry from head to toe. "All done with Tister," he announced proudly.

Before climbing down from the stool, his powdery hands reached for a peanut butter sandwich on a nearby dish. Denny walked into the kitchen and, surveying their latest production, howled with laughter. "So where did the baby ghost come from?"

Marge pointed to Barry as she tilted her head in question. "You're home early?"

"I'm caught up at the office. I thought I'd play a game of baseball with Barry."

Upon hearing the word *baseball*, Barry crammed the rest of his sandwich into his mouth and, with his mouth full, exclaimed, "I can bop the ball far away, Daddy. All the way up to the sun, even past my swing set."

While feeding Sherry, Marge watched Barry bat the ball. He was extremely well-coordinated. Suddenly he dropped his small bat and held his left ear. "Hurts," he cried. "Hurts!"

After returning Sherry to her baby seat, Marge rushed outside. Denny was bending beside Barry, examining his ear. A familiar look of concern had turned earlier smiles into a frown. "This can't go on," he said.

"I know. It's ridiculous." As she checked for a fever, she was reminded that these constant ear infections were a blemish to an almost unmarred life for Barry. The dilemma of Barry's feet and hearing loss had been dealt with. This, together with their marital problems solved, seemed to have wiped the slate clean. Still examining Barry's ears, Marge noted in his expression the innocence of one untouched by time, whose eyes were unclouded by failure or fear. He was so full of life. She had hoped beyond hope that his hearing loss was their only mountain left to conquer. However, she knew that part of his hearing loss was due to constant ear infections and high fevers that came on suddenly.

"Did you tell the doctor that the earaches are continuing?" Denny questioned.

"Constantly. Before Sherry was born, he told me that if Barry wasn't an only child, I wouldn't notice him so much. I retaliated by saying I wasn't making up his 103 degrees temperature."

"Well, Barry is *not* an only child!" Denny responded angrily. "It's time to find another doctor."

Marge totally agreed. Turning to Barry, she said, "Mommy's going to call a new doctor, baby. One who'll make your pain go away."

"Boo-boo hurts," Barry cried. "Fix it."

A trio of doctors were recommended. Pleading that it was an emergency situation, Marge was told they could work Barry in. As she and Barry waited in the examination room, one particular doctor stood in the doorway three different times. Each time he looked at Barry intently but said nothing. The fourth time the doctor walked into the room and introduced himself. "I'm Dr. Saltzman."

After examining Barry's ears, he said that he thought he could take care of Barry's constant ear infections. "I'd like to see you in my office," he added in a tone that in no way offered relief.

Once seated behind his desk, Dr. Saltzman said, "I suspect what the underlying problem is, but I'm not qualified to make a definite diagnosis. Would you be willing to go to the hospital tomorrow for tests?"

Grateful that someone was taking extra steps to pinpoint Barry's problem, Marge responded with an enthusiastic yes.

"Good," Dr. Saltzman replied as he telephoned the hospital. "Can you be there by one thirty?" he asked. Marge nodded. Dr. Saltzman handed her a list of instructions then added, "After the tests, I'd like to see you back in my office around four o'clock." Again Marge nodded.

It was too beautiful an afternoon to spend waiting in an X-ray room at a hospital, but what had to be done had to be done. She had no idea what the extent of the tests meant, and her curiosity was mounting, especially after Barry's entire body was X-rayed. When she was asked if they could do a second set of X-rays, threatening clouds of fear darkened her mind.

"We need to do a third set," a technician informed her after another lengthy wait.

As her fears grew, she attempted to draw upon faith to keep her from returning to a world of doubt, but old habits were hard to break. "Why the same tests three times? Aren't the other tests turning out?"

"Yes," the technician answered.

"Is Barry moving around too much?"

"No."

"Then why the same X-rays over and over again?"

For a brief moment, the technician lowered his eyes. "Dr. Saltzman will explain it to you at his office today."

Rushing from the hospital to Dr. Saltzman's office, Marge apologized for being late. "I'm so sorry. It's almost five thirty, but the hospital insisted on retaking tests. I've no idea what went wrong."

"Calm down," Dr. Saltzman soothed. "I know exactly how long the tests took. The hospital called every thirty minutes."

Marge felt her heart freeze. "Oh, dear God, what now?"

Not responding to her terror, Dr. Saltzman explained that he wanted to make arrangements for Barry to go to the University of Florida Shands Teaching Hospital in Gainesville, Florida. "You'll need to go with him. The tests will take a week."

Marge had no idea what any of this meant and, in an odd way, didn't want to pursue with additional questions. "When do you want us to go?" she asked weakly.

"The sooner the better, Mrs. Glider. I'll make all of the necessary arrangements with Dr. Andrew Lorincz. He'll meet you at Shands. So that you and Barry can share a room, you'll both be admitted as patients."

Marge was confused.

"There's another reason why we need you admitted as a patient," the doctor added. "We'll need to put you through every test we give Barry."

"What kind of tests?"

"X-rays, blood tests, family history charts."

"Why?" Marge asked, looking at him with bewilderment.

Dr. Saltzman's voice was shaded with caution as he replied, "To see if there's a genetic link."

Marge let his response pass without comment. Again, it was as if she were afraid to probe too deeply. Instead she convinced herself that these extensive tests were little more than a thorough physical examination—tests that would isolate the root problem of Barry's constant ear infections and thus a medical cure would be found.

That's all there was to it. Nothing more.

Kay agreed to care for Sherry for as long as needed. Denny would drive them to Shands where he would leave them there and then return home in order to work. As they began the five-to-six-hour drive from Miami to Gainesville, neither Marge nor Denny dared to put into words the silent fears smothering them. Instead they spoke in artificial tones about the weather and other safe topics, pausing every so often to laugh at Barry who found the trip an unexpected adventure.

"I go bye-bye to somewhere," Barry sang. "Far, far away to somewhere, to somewhere, to somewhere…"

Marge pulled from her handbag the instruction sheet Dr. Saltzman had given her to bring to Shands. A word was underlined, followed by a question mark: _Hurlers?_

Before leaving them at Shands, Denny told her that everything would be fine, that at last they would find what was causing Barry's constant earaches and fevers.

In between tests, Marge took Barry's hand, and they explored the huge hospital, ending up in the cafeteria where Barry was treated to red Jell-O with whipped cream. Their hospital explorations were so frequent that many of the nurses and doctors recognized Barry to the point of greeting him by name. Yet despite the fact everyone treated them well, Marge's terror continued to mount. It was the type of terror that could find no relief in words.

When she and Barry were alone in their hospital room at night, she found herself staring at her little boy with a sense of total and undefinable desolation. "Do you want Mommy to read you a story?" she asked as she sat on the edge of his bed.

Barry's smile was instant.

In the middle of her reading, she stopped in order to hug him, then touch his cheek. "I love you, Little Boop."

Snuggling comfortably beneath his covers, Barry reached up and touched her cheek. "Love you too, Mommy."

Marge felt her heart breaking. She wanted to hold Barry close and never let him go. Perhaps if she kept hugging and loving him, everything *would* turn out fine. As she bent forward again, Barry pulled back. "Hug all done, Mommy. Read my story again," he said innocently.

Marge looked flustered and relieved as she began, "Once upon a time..."

After a week of enduring every test possible, Dr. Lorincz asked her to come to his office.

"Have you found out what's causing Barry's ear infections?" she asked.

So much silence filled the room that the ticking of a wall clock was magnified. Finally, Dr. Lorincz spoke. His words were slow and measured. "Mrs. Glider, we need your husband here with you."

Marge's legs went weak as a sense of déjà vu came over her. "You *need* Denny here before you can tell me the results of the tests?"

"Yes." Dr. Lorincz paused and closed his eyes. When he lifted them, his voice held compassion. "Would you ask him to meet with me tomorrow if possible?"

By the time Denny flew in the next afternoon, Marge was physically and spiritually fatigued. It had never occurred to her that it was possible to feel so tired and so empty. It was an exhaustion that drained her soul. Seeing Denny, she detected in him a sadness that made his once inexhaustible spirit equally weary.

As they sat waiting in Dr. Lorincz's office for their appointed meeting, they tried not to look at each other. The waiting was raw and labored. Marge kept telling herself nothing was seriously wrong. The worst—the very *worst* that could happen—would be to learn that Barry's hearing was deteriorating. Her fears were the result of thinking with her emotions rather than with her mind.

When nothing she said to herself worked, she decided to stop thinking altogether.

Despite the afternoon's bright sunlight pouring in through a window, Dr. Lorincz's face was the face of darkness. His voice was hushed and sorrowful. Rather than address the issue of Barry's tests, he began by talking to them about their marriage. "Your marriage is going to be challenged in ways you cannot imagine," he said.

Marge and Denny looked at each other. Neither were used to having their personal life placed under a microscope. Dr. Lorincz's opening statement shook them so profoundly that they sensed they were only a breath away from crumbling. Marge continued staring at Denny to see if he understood something she didn't. What she saw on Denny's face was not understanding but bewilderment.

Dr. Lorincz, his hands folded over manila files, leaned toward them in a gesture that suggested familiarity. "In addition to Barry, you have a baby daughter. There's going to be a time, Mrs. Glider, when you'll have to choose between Barry, your husband, and your little girl."

Marge looked at the doctor with a disbelief that turned to terror. She felt a knife cut into her heart. What was happening? What was Dr. Lorincz trying to tell them?

Denny sat in stunned silence. He turned his head toward the window and incredulously thought it was unseasonably hot for October, and like him, the earth itself seemed to be gasping for breath. With their hearts fumbling for relief, their eyes pleaded for Dr. Lorincz to tell them a truth they did not want to hear.

Dr. Lorincz tapped the files on his desk. His hesitancy about continuing was apparent. Searching for his voice, he finally said, "Barry has a genetic disorder called Hurler syndrome. Hurler is a rare disease that occurs in about a half million births. It's not widely known. It's so rare it can be recessive for four or five generations. It's quite difficult to diagnose because it can take so many unexpected turns. Mental regression usually takes place around five years of age coincided by the loss of most physical capacities. No amount of love or care is going to prevent what will happen to Barry from happening."

Marge and Denny drew back as if struck by lightning. Each tried to command their voice to speak, but no sound was possible.

Dr. Lorincz behaved with kindness, while the meaning of his words grew more and more brutal. "To repeat, no amount of love or care can prevent what is going to happen to Barry. To save your marriage, to care for your baby daughter, Barry may have to be institutionalized at some future time. He'll become extremely hyperactive to the point of uncontrollable running and yelling."

Marge put her head into her hands. She needed to run from this, to *not* listen to this!

"Taking care of Barry will be the equivalent of raising five children. He'll regress daily."

Marge removed her hands in order that her eyes plead with Denny. He said nothing. His face was white, and his expression frozen. Even his eyes were drained of color.

Dr. Lorincz cleared his throat. What he must say now, he must say quickly. "The average age of death is around ten years of age."

Stunned beyond belief, it was Denny who first found his voice. "*Death?* Are you saying Barry is dying? How can that be? My son's *only* three years old. He's full of life, smart. This isn't possible…"

Marge felt as if she would collapse. None of this could be true. This had to be some terrible, horrible nightmare!

Dr. Lorincz felt his heart fill with grief. "There's a 5 percent chance Barry could escape regression. When this happens, these children are highly intelligent and very normal."

Struggling not to fall apart, Marge grabbed for whatever glimmer of hope was available. "Barry's extremely smart. Maybe this is a clue that Barry will fall within that 5 percent range, or maybe between now and then, a cure will be found."

"Perhaps," Dr. Lorincz said with quiet skepticism. "We're already looking for a cure. As for the 5 percent range, we'll know if this is true when Barry's around five years of age—the age when the first signs of regression begin to appear. In the meantime, I want you to keep a journal on Barry's progress. We'd like to see him for tests every six months. As you know, there will be no cost to you. Shands is part of a government research grant program established to find a cure for Hurler syndrome. The grant money will pay for all of Barry's tests as well as enabling him to enter into our research program. Whatever occurs, you'll not have the additional burden of the expenses associated with Barry's disease."

Knowing that their entire world was disintegrating, Marge wondered if her heart would ever smile again. This had to be a nightmare from which she would soon awaken!

It had to be!

"Very little is known about this disease," Dr. Lorincz explained as he handed them a small booklet to study. "Dr. Harold Schei is a physician who wrote extensively about Hurler's a few years ago, although there are records that date back as far as 1900. Hurler syndrome is an inherited rare genetic disease largely of the bones. Dwarfism and other skeletal deformities begin to appear, deafness, clouding of the cornea, enlargement of the liver and spleen, abnormalities of the heart, ruptures, and limited joint motion occur. The skin may become hairy in places. There may be rough places and nodules on the skin, and perhaps some ulcers will appear on the thickening skin of the hands."

As black confusion continued to mount, Marge fumbled for words of hope. Barry, playing happily with some toys on the office rug, paid no attention to the drama surrounding his existence. "This is impossible. You have to be wrong!" Marge cried out.

"I want to be wrong," Dr. Lorincz replied. "I pray I am."

"You have to be! Look at Barry. He's so beautiful, so smart. How can he lose what he already has? I don't understand..."

Dr. Lorincz's voice remained steady. "Shands has the best testing facilities available. Extreme caution is taken, which is why so many tests were redone. We had to be sure. Unfortunately, mental retardation coincides with the changes I outlined."

"How can this happen?" she cried, astounded.

"This occurs because of the abnormalities in the chemistry of the body."

"Yet there's a possibility that Barry could fall into the 5 percent who survive?"

With as much understanding as possible, Dr. Lorincz looked at this young couple in their twenties. He recognized their strength and their fear and especially their hope that was desperately struggling to survive. Their world had been shattered. Their son would become a human guinea pig in a government research program. Sadly, he had to be the one to tell them that their precious little boy would die, and in his dying, a part of them would die. He would have to watch their faith shatter and their soul brought to tears. He wanted to tell them that there was nothing they could do about it except go through it.

And he would tell them that. But not today, not today.

*****

A mother's memory of her five-year-old son

"Mommy, guess what I finded out today?"

"What, Barry?"

"I finded out that you can't save a popsicle by hiding it 'neath your pillow."

10

In the Quiet

Out of suffering have emerged the strongest souls; the
most massive characters are seared with scars.

—E.H. Chapin

"Did you say something?" Denny asked.

"No," she whispered again.

In feverish and shocked silence, Marge and Denny began their
long drive home. Their expectations of a remedy for Barry's ear infections had been shattered.

*Their little boy was going to die. And before he died, he was going
to suffer.*

Unconsciously Marge clutched at one of Barry's blankets that
had found its way to the front seat of the car. Her breathing was
labored, as was Denny's. Each seemed to be waiting for the other to
speak, but their devastation was so deep that they were incapable of
voicing thoughts—each was silently trying to comprehend the truth
that their world had disintegrated. Absolutely nothing in their life
had prepared them for this.

Marge's shock continued to pace the floor of her mind in search
for an escape from the most hideous of nightmares. She was frantically seeking some ray of hope that would lighten the darkness par-
alyzing her soul. Despite her disorientation, flashes of comforting

memories added their own contour: Barry's ice-cream-covered face, his joy at seeing his first tricycle, the occasional cowlick she smoothed back, the Halloween where he wore his favorite cowboy suit, and the many hugs and kisses.

Denny's mind also traveled backward: Barry hopping up on a stool to sit beside him at the breakfast bar asking for a cup of "kaukee." Pouring juice in a mug that matched his own, he would wink at Marge and say, "Barry and I are discussing events over coffee."

It may be they would never share coffee together.

If not for driving, he would have put his head down on the steering wheel and cried. His only son was dying from a rare disease that had no cure—a disease that before ending his life would first debilitate his mind and his body. None of this was real. It could *not* be happening. Denny glanced in the rearview mirror. Barry appeared healthy. How could he be facing a death sentence? How could all of his hopes and dreams for his son have been dashed like a ship against a rocky shore? How could his family be drowning in a raging sea of helplessness with his having no idea how to save them? Still, even though the doctors had not wanted to present false hopes, there was that 5 percent chance that Barry might outwit the disease—a remote chance worth clinging to. He would pray for a miracle, pray that God would help Barry beat the statistics. He had to be strong for Marge, Barry, and Sherry. Being strong meant *not* to cry, but it did not mean *not* to pray. He was praying with his heart and his soul, and he would continue praying. God would hear his prayers.

He had to.

Leaning her head slightly against the car window, Marge closed her eyes as her memory continued backward: She had just given birth to Barry and had been told about his club feet. It was as if she were standing outside her hospital room, slowly walking toward it as if in a floating motion. Then she was in bed and, in a voice slow and hazy, asked Betty Jo, "*Why* are you telling me this?"

These children are God's special angels. We are all born for a purpose. It is the same with everyone. The mind is eternal. In living the human experience, these children show us the spiritual experience. Birth is when the breath begins and the mind is imprisoned. Ironically, death is when the breath stops and the mind is set free. Through death, one is truly born again.

Opening her eyes, Marge saw her image captured in the glass of the car window. For a moment, it seemed she could see Betty Jo's image as well, yet as she searched further, the image disappeared. Allowing what was unfolding in her mind to take its own path, she sensed the urgency of replacing fear with a reawakening, and as she did, the memory of Barry's past—his club feet and earaches—faded. In its place was an intelligent little boy with blue eyes. He was batting a ball tossed to him by Denny, who was saying, "It won't be long until I can take him to a major league game. Heck, I wouldn't be surprised if someday he turns out to be a pro player."

Within this image-mixing, another door of memory burst open: Barry's recent dedication at the Baptist church and the little white Bible presented to him. Suddenly the event took on new meaning. Stymied, Marge mentally stepped back in order to examine what this interpretation meant, almost as if at a distance a clue would be revealed. She remembered word for word the writing on Barry's Certificate of Dedication:

> Barry Eugene Glider was born November 7, 1963, and was presented to the Lord in Dedication by Mr. and Mrs. Dennis G. Glider.

Alongside the dedication appeared the words:

> *Suffer the little children to come onto me and forbid them not; for such is the kingdom of heaven.*

There was a hint of irony in this particular memory: they had given Barry away that day but could not have fathomed that God would collect him so soon.

The good memories and the reality of what could happen to Barry conspired against her in a way that made her clutch Barry's misplaced blanket. She was delirious with pain as she silently pleaded, *Oh, Lord, why? Please, dear Lord, why us, why our baby?*

Barry, playing in the back seat, was wonderfully oblivious to the death sentence handed him. Filled with childish bounce, he sang his song: "Going bye-bye to somewhere, to somewhere, to somewhere." Ceasing his singing, he pointed out the window with impish glee. "B-i-i-g tuck, Mommy!" he announced excitedly when a large red truck passed by. As he prattled these words in childish sequence, he adjusted his cowboy hat; and while pretending to be riding a horse, he took aim with his right hand and yelled, "*Bang-bang.*"

Attempting to clear her head, Marge turned and, seeing Barry's face puckered into a huge smile, felt her eyes swell with tears. Nothing had changed with him. He was still their Barry, still smart, still eager to learn and pretend. Unable to take her eyes off Barry's face, the tears rolled down her cheeks.

"Have a boo-boo, Mommy?" Barry asked as he reached out to touch her tears, then drawing his hand back, he kissed his own fingers and stretched forward in order to plant a finger-kiss upon her cheek. "Me fix boo-boo."

Denny reached over and squeezed Marge's hand. "Barry's highly intelligent and normal. He's going to make it, honey. He's got to."

With the silence broken, they began exchanging questions and answers. But beneath a charade of normalcy, the fear remained, and no amount of hope could erase this. They each realized that there was no punishment in the world quite as painful as repeated lies, even if done in the name of giving to the other false hope. Each knew they were galloping around the edges of reality by pretending their nightmare was one they would soon awake from.

As Barry resumed his singsong, Marge hummed along with him. Momentarily this brought about a sense of peace that further words would only eliminate. In the humming, there was also a sense of hope that said, "*When words are forgotten the melody continues on.*"

Their life became a series of two steps forward, one step backward, with fear being conquered one step at a time. Their shock was so deep that at first it was impossible for them to find the courage to tell their families that Barry might die. Instead, it became easier to explain Barry's disease while eliminating its possible end result. On the other hand, Marge knew her parents no doubt guessed the truth in the way Barry became more precious to them. It was simply that their hearts could not accept any truth that had *final* attached to it. When they finally discussed everything openly, the discussion was colored by the belief that Barry *would* indeed be part of that 5 percent who beat the odds.

Blessedly being the mother of a baby girl and an active three-year-old did not allow much time for doubt to rule Marge's mind. It was only when both children were asleep and when she dozed off that she often awakened with a start. Whether alone or trying not to wake Denny, she would lay quietly curled up with her face pressed into her pillow and cry, *"No..."*

Eleven months later, when Barry was four and Sherry was a year old, Denny rushed into the house calling for her. In his hand, he carried a sheaf of papers that he was waving as though a flag. "I've been offered a promotion in Atlanta, Georgia!" he shouted.

"Atlanta? I loved Atlanta when we visited there," she responded with equal excitement.

"Then it's all right?" Denny asked.

Marge laughed. "I think it's a godsend, Denny. It's getting so crowded here, and so many of the newcomers are loud and rude. Plus with Kay and Sonny having recently moved to Charlotte, North Carolina, we'll be closer to them."

Denny's face filled with relief. "I'm going to make at least a hundred dollars more a month, plus the company will move us. I also found out that if we live in DeKalb County they have one of the finest special education programs in the south for Barry."

Sprinkled between an almost inexhaustible amount of planning, a mutual and spontaneous joy exploded in them—an omen of good things coming their way. Perhaps their storm had passed and the clouds had parted. Plus, neither she nor Denny had noticed the tiniest change in Barry other than a forward progression. Even the ear infections and high fevers had disappeared. The only drawback was that Barry would not get to see his grandparents as often as before, particularly Marge's parents who had moved to be near them. "I don't know how I'm going to tell Mother and Daddy," Marge said to Denny. "You know how much Barry and Sherry love their grandma and grandpa."

Denny smiled. "At least you won't get irritated at your father for dropping by at five and spoiling Barry's dinner by taking him out for an ice cream cone."

"No, but I will miss Mother taking care of Sherry for the trips to Shands and Daddy taking Barry on Saturday morning pony rides at the ring. Of course, Sherry won't miss the rides since she screams every time she's put on a pony, which totally befuddles Barry. He can't imagine anyone *not* liking a horse, even if it's only a pony."

Stone Mountain, known for its six hundred and fifty-foot-high granite dome, sat in northwest Georgia, a few miles northeast of Atlanta. Sculptured into the northern face of Stone Mountain were the equestrian figures of Robert E. Lee, Stonewall Jackson, and Jefferson Davis. The only drawback to the move to Georgia was its winter climate. They had few cold-weather clothing. In fact, they had to borrow a pink snowsuit for Sherry for the car trip north. Luckily Denny's company agreed to pay the mortgage on their Florida home until it sold, which could take a while since Florida was suffering a depression. Another bonus was that their new house was located in DeKalb County. They would be moving into a two-year-old white brick split level accented by blue shutters. The roomy house had hardwood floors and large airy windows through which she could view the hills and mountains, each offering a sense of strength and eternity. Having left the company car behind in Florida in favor of picking another one up in Atlanta, the trip had turned into a family vacation. While Sherry napped, Barry could barely contain his excitement. To him the move did not mean leaving Grandma and Grandpa but was instead another grand adventure. When the giant granite came into view, Barry drew to his knees, and his eyes widened as he took in the stone's massive carvings. "What's *that*, Mommy?"

"That's Stone Mountain," Marge explained.

Barry shook his head. "Noooo, that's b-i-i-g horseys!"

Tired and happy, they tucked the children into their makeshift beds in their new home. Tomorrow the moving van would arrive.

Snuggling against Denny, Marge said, "This move has made me feel stronger and much more hopeful."

"Me too," Denny admitted before falling into much-needed sleep. An hour later, Denny began moaning uncomfortably. As Marge watched the nightmare work its way across his face, she considered wakening him but decided against it. It was not necessary for her to ask *what* his nightmare was about.

*****

A mother's memory of her five-year-old son

"Mommy, guess what I finded out today?"

"What, Barry?"

"I finded out that peas sink to the bottom of the potty."

11

Hope

Hope is the pillar that holds up the world.
Hope is the dream of a waking man.

—Pliny the Elder (AD 23–79)

Marge knew that if either she or Denny truly lost hope, they might not be able to carry on. Hope was like a powerful tonic that strengthened them for tomorrow and gave them the courage to see sunshine behind the clouds rather than the shadows of an evergrowing storm.

With moving boxes still cluttering the floors of various rooms of their new home, Marge looked around. She was irresistibly drawn toward three shafts of sunrays filtering in through an undraped window. Moved by the breeze, the rays took on the shape of a cross. For a few seconds, the cross stood visible and brilliant, as though physically injecting spiritual hope into their lives. A lump of gratitude tightened her throat, and as her hands unconsciously clasped together in prayer, she felt an unmistakable power embrace her.

She was *not* alone.

Exhausted from the trip, Barry and Sherry were napping when Denny walked in and began surveying the various boxes waiting to be unpacked. Something prevented her from pointing toward the cross, which in the final analysis was best. The cross had disappeared. For a second, she wondered if it had simply been a figment of her imagination. She didn't want to appear as so unrealistic that she was projecting false images wrapped around false hopes. Taking control of reality, she turned to Denny and told him that they needed to find a five-day-a-week preschool program for four-year-olds. "Barry's still behind in his speech, but I think if he's with other children, his development will improve."

Denny remained thoughtful as his lean hands began untaping one of the boxes. "Marge," he said, "do you think Barry'll fit in? Be accepted?" When he saw her face contract with anxiety, he added, "What I'm trying to say is that other children can be cruel. I don't want Barry made fun of."

As various apprehensions swept through, Marge remembered the shaft of sun that had taken on the shape of a cross. "We can't postpone the inevitable, Denny. Barry loves other children, and even if his speech is not at their level, don't you think his loving nature will draw others to him?"

Denny nodded as he followed her to the large kitchen. Its white counters and beautiful green stained cabinets was their favorite room. It sat four steps higher than the spacious den with its paneling stained the same green as the kitchen. The kitchen was unlike anyone else's since it had been built with so many extras, which included forty-two cabinets. While Marge prepared a light lunch, they discussed Barry, the end result being his enrollment in a four-year-old kindergarten as soon as possible. "It's a private school," Marge explained, "which means added expense."

Denny nodded. "Barry needs it. We'll manage somehow." He paused. "After all, we've managed everything so far. Plus, Barry has adapted well to our move here. He'll adapt to the adventure of this new school. I'm positive he will."

Because Denny was traveling from Monday through Thursday, Marge had daily talks with the teacher that first month to be sure Barry was okay. Her apprehension was greatly lessened when Barry's teacher told her that he mixed well with other children. "He's accepted by the other children and doesn't realize he's different at all," Marge told Denny. "I've explained to everyone at school what Barry's problem is, that we're hoping for the best, that the future would have to be faced one day at a time."

Denny was relieved. "I think it was Abraham Lincoln who said the best thing about the future is that it comes *only* one day at a time."

Their second ray of comfort was when they noticed an improvement in Barry's overall behavior. "He still has temper tantrums now and then and can be as stubborn as a mule," she elaborated. "But that's normal for a boy. My friends say this describes their children as well."

"That's great," Denny answered, not concealing the pleasure he felt. "Plus he's getting better and better at hitting and pitching a baseball. You know, Marge, Barry hits the ball much better than older kids. He's really coordinated." Pausing in his list of superlatives, Denny's voice took on the ring of every other father who proudly reviews their male offspring. Hailing his son as baseball's next "discovery," Denny told Marge, "Hand-eye coordination is a clear sign of mental agility. Barry's definitely progressing forward, *not* backward."

Hearing words of praise for Barry was magic to Marge's ears. "Have you seen the way Barry dances? He's even trying to tap dance. He loves music, and he's extremely good at working puzzles too. That requires a lot of mental discipline, especially in a child so young."

Intoxicated by Barry's achievements, they scurried from one act of praise to another, each achievement meant that not only was everything all right, but also that their son actually was superior to other boys his age.

By the time Barry reached his fifth birthday, Marge began to relax. During this time, they made new friends, as well as receiving visits from old friends, including Sandy and Roy Wilson, who were also moving to Georgia. Roy stayed with them until he found a house and got his family moved. When Christmas vacation came, Barry's teacher asked for a conference. With Denny traveling, Marge attended alone. She was totally unprepared for what was to occur.

"Barry's become very disruptive," Barry's teacher informed her. "He's hyperactive. He walks, talks, and screams anytime or anywhere he feels like it. He won't do anything I ask him to, only what he wants to do, *when* he wants to do it. My inability to control him destroys my control over the entire class."

Shock and confusion sank in. After looking frantically around the room, Marge stared at the teacher. "I don't understand. Last month you told me everything was fine."

"It was. But now it's not. Barry's out of control, Mrs. Glider. I'm sorry, I really am," she said sadly. "I don't know what to do with Barry. It's not fair to the other children to have one child behave so disruptively. I'm afraid he'll have to be removed."

"Removed?"

"Yes. He cannot return after Christmas."

Marge felt so drained that her knees grew weak. The teacher's indictment was a total shock. Stammering out something through strained lips, Marge's mind recoiled as Dr. Lorincz's predictions sank through: *Mental regression usually takes place around five years of age. Barry will become extremely hyperactive to the point of disruption. He'll regress daily.* Next came the words she could not bear to hear repeated, *This will be coincided by the loss of all physical capacities until the body dies.*

Hope suddenly became a stranger. Yet to *not* hope would be to cast them into an eternal pit of despair. This could *not* mean that Barry would not be a part of that 5 percent who survived, and if he was not, then a cure was just around the corner.

It had to be!

No matter, Barry must receive training in order to progress. To that end, they petitioned the DeKalb County School Board to allow Barry to enter the public-school system. Since Barry was five and not six, they were refused.

"We can't take no for an answer," Marge told Denny. "Not only does Barry love being with other children, but he *needs* to be with other children. His future is at stake."

Denny's fervor matched Marge's. "Then we keep petitioning the board until they say yes." It was also the way he attacked life in general. With persistence, they were told that Barry could enter the Educatable Program at Indian Creek Elementary School in Stone Mountain the following March.

The first day was a disaster. When the principal called Marge at home, he said, "Not only is Barry refusing to sit, but he's had a temper tantrum, has kicked the teacher, and has turned over a desk."

Rushing to the school, Marge wondered if the teacher had tried to physically force Barry to sit? After all, Barry had never been violent before. Surely in the school's history, there had been other children—children *without* Hurler's—who had temper tantrums. Fortunately, the teacher agreed to allow Barry to return the next day. Although there were no more incidents of that nature, the school complained of other disruptions. Sometimes Barry wet his pants, and although he had another pair with him, the school would insist Marge, with two-year-old Sherry in tow, drive over and change him. Marge wanted to remind them that five-year-olds often had "wetting accidents." But fearing that if she made waves, Barry would be asked to leave, so she kept silent. Plus the positives were that Barry had begun to learn how to write his name and the alphabet, each in proper sequence.

By the end of April, Marge noted Barry had left off a letter from his ABCs. The following week, two or three more letters were dropped. By May, Barry could not remember what a pencil was for.

Barry will regress daily, Dr. Lorincz had warned.

Alone at night, Marge sat in her bedroom numb with grief. She wanted to talk to Denny, but what was there to say? *It* had come. And with *its* arrival, all their hopes were being trampled beneath a crushing disease that held no mercy.

With the mental regression came wildness. There were times when Barry would reach the height of his frustrations and scream wildly, as though trying to break through the walls of a body both crippling and imprisoning. It seemed his unresting body was trying to compensate for a mind that was day-by-day entering into a sleep from which it would never awaken.

Other times, Barry would deliberately bend her fingers in a backward position or stomp violently on her foot. "His mind is losing ground," she cried to Denny. "But his strength and hyperactivity are radically increasing. He's so strong. I only outwit him because I'm smarter."

Realizing that Marge had become a victim of Barry's disease, Denny had no idea what to do. He never wanted to holler or spank Barry, but he didn't know what else to do.

"Stop lashing out at Barry," Marge shouted with an evergrowing hysteria. "He doesn't mean to do these things. He's not disobedient. Dear God, Denny, he's sick!"

"And what about his fascination with knives?" Denny shouted back with equal frustration. "What if he hurts Sherry or you?"

"I've locked the knives away in the bread box."

"And do you intend to lock Sherry away in a bread box as well?" Denny's voice reduced to helplessness. "Sherry's our child too. Doesn't she deserve some safety, some peace? Or maybe we should all lock ourselves away and let Barry have the run of the house." Denny's eyes shifted from anger to frustration. How was it possible to cure the incurable? He loved Marge, he loved Sherry, and he loved Barry—*this* Barry as well as the other Barry. Still, what were they going to do with this *new* Barry—this wild, destructive Barry? "Marge," Denny said in a calm voice, "Barry's not even allowed to return to the Educatable Program anymore."

"They're going to accept him in the Trainable Program next fall," she reminded.

"Yes, but if he continues in this undisciplined mode, he'll be kicked out of there as well." Shaking his head futilely, Denny felt his temper once more rise to the surface. "Damn! *Someone* has to sit on that boy!"

Marge shook her head helplessly. She experienced an unutterable anger toward Denny that went beyond Barry's actions. With mounting bills, Denny had to work longer and harder thus leaving more of the responsibility of raising the children with her. Medication after medication was tried on Barry, but nothing worked longer than a few weeks. There were the trips to Shands followed by Barry's downward spiral into fury. Yet despite all of this, they still held tight to a glimmer of hope—*that a cure would be found.*

Each day Marge found resentment rising, and despite knowing *why* Denny had to work so long and so hard, he at least had the freedom to open the door in the morning and leave the chaos behind.

When he returned at night, he was insistent that the abnormal appear normal—that by force he could *make* Barry behave, when in truth, their son's problems had nothing whatsoever to do with willful misbehavior.

Battle lines had been drawn with her as hostage.

The taste of acrid bitterness was on her tongue when she lashed out, "Why do you even bother coming home, Denny? It's easier without you. You should be making things better for us, not worse." Turning, she ran to her bedroom and threw herself on the bed. Drawing into a fetal position, she covered her ears. She wanted to turn the sounds of life "off."

But she couldn't. *There's going to be a time when you'll have to choose between Barry, your husband, and your little girl.*

No, she pleaded. *I can't! I'm Barry's mother!*

As her tears magnified the sound of silence, she knew she was being hurled into a downward plunge where hope was simply an afterthought.

Sitting at the kitchen table, as though to deliberately accentuate his mother's utter helplessness while at the same time challenging his father's need for discipline, Barry swept his arm across the table and, with sudden and frantic movements, knocked his dinner—and theirs—violently to the floor.

*****

A mother's memory of her five-year-old son

"Mommy, guess what I finded out today?"

"What, Barry?"

"I finded out that Grandmas who wear a Mickey Mouse watch laugh a lot."

12

No Daylight

I want to know if I can live with what I know, and only that.

—Albert Camus

The summer before entering the trainable program was the last summer Barry was even remotely responsible. He loved to go outside and play on his swing set or sit in a little plastic swimming pool. Although he was regressing into a baby, his eyes were always full of love and trust; they held no fear whatsoever. Perhaps something deep in his soul declared that the love he gave would in the end bring about enough love that might cure.

Many afternoons were spent playing in the shallow creek at Stone Mountain Park. Marge sat in the creek in a lawn chair with her feet in the cool waters, protecting Barry and Sherry as they laughingly splashed about. When looking at Barry, it was times such as those that life seemed normal. Only it was not normal: almost overnight, Barry no longer knew how to write any of his letters but instead would repeatedly scribble straight lines up and down over the paper. Because he had lost his two front bottom teeth, he was chewing and biting everything in sight: tabletops, windowsills, chairs, and his toys. All toilet training reversed, and he now wet in his pants as a baby would. The many years that Barry had been able to dress himself also reversed. He had no idea what to do. Sometimes he put his underwear on over his pants or in other instances would walk around the house with his underpants in his hand. Comprehension and logic were disappearing at such an alarming rate that what now stood in place of a once brilliant child was an overgrown baby with a blank stare. He no longer knew what he was doing or what he was *not* doing. A disaster almost occurred when they had recently taken a family camping trip, something they had done in the past and some-thing Barry had totally enjoyed. With their little camper set up in a South Georgia park, Denny had built a bonfire the first night for the traditional roasting of marshmallows. Having disappeared for a few minutes and leaving Barry with Marge, Marge had also turned her back. When she turned back, Barry was standing in the middle of the fire! Because his rescue was so immediate, he wasn't burned, but it left Denny and Marge's nerves shattered to the point they knew that reasoning had totally disappeared from Barry's brain—that danger loomed everywhere.

They returned home at daybreak.

Totally frightened, Marge sent a written report to Shands:

> Barry now has no responsibility about any-thing whereas before I could always depend on him to perform and complete simple errands or instructions. He has also begun violently fighting me if I make any effort to touch him. His tem-per has tremendously increased and the behavior is so infantile it's like having a sixty pound, six-year-old baby. Barry is very strong and constantly hurts our dog by squeezing or pulling parts of her, and he will always try to bend back my fin-gernails and fingers anytime he can get my hand. I honestly don't believe he intends to do 99% of the things he does, but he just doesn't understand himself. We still discipline, of course, but it has very little effect. Could you please tell us what a Hurlers regression is like—any advice would be

greatly appreciated. I will await your reply as I need some help desperately.

No one in the medical community had an answer, only compassion. They knew, as did she and Denny, that slowly, like a cassette tape wound backward, Barry's mind was being erased each night.

At the end of June, Barry was admitted into a summer day camp in relation to the new school for the trainable mentally retarded. There were one hundred children admitted into a program geared and designed toward each child's ability. Prior to attendance, Barry was tested on his speech-language abilities by the Dekalb County Board of Education.

Speech

> Errors consisted of substitution and omissions. Examiner unable to get Barry to imitate any of his sound errors. Barry refused to allow the evaluator to examine the oral mechanism.

Language

> On the Peabody Picture Vocabulary Test, Barry scored 2 years and 4 months in receptive vocabulary. On the Myklebust Language Scale he scored approximately 3 years in expressive language.

On June 24, 1960, Barry was given the Illinois Test of Psycholinguistic Abilities. He earned an overall language age of three years and five months. His range of scores was two years and two months to five years and zero month. His strengths were in visual closure and visual association. His weaknesses were in auditory reception, auditory association, verbal expression, auditory memory, and grammatic closure.

The final comments of the staff were:

> We are of the opinion that Barry's major difficulty lies within the mental retardation rather than the hearing aspect, resulting in a definite language delay. Therefore, the best educational placement would be in a small classroom for educable mentally retarded children with major emphasis on language development.

Seeing the results of Barry's testing in black and white left Marge staring at the past with a pain that was nearly unbearable. In her mind, she could see Barry's intelligent eyes and quick ability to learn; could see the little boy who once proudly wrote his name, who drew pictures, and who used his hands to hug, not to hurt. As these now-gone memories circled around her, the pale light of the sun fell on Barry, who remained staring at her with fearless, yet trusting, eyes.

Denny wrote Dr. Lorincz his own comments:

> As you know Barry had signs of an internal hernia in his groin which had not previously given him any trouble. However, a month ago it burst and extends approximately 3 to 4 inches, completely filling his right testicle and extending upward into the groin. There was some swelling the first week, but it subsided and is now only a hard lump, which he complains hurts him. We know how you feel concerning operative procedures on small children, but in light of the situation we are inquiring as to what you feel is the best course to follow.
>
> We would like, with your concurrence, to have it taken care of before school starts. If we do proceed with correcting this problem, would it be possible to correct his umbilical hernia at the same time? We could have this done in Atlanta.

However, you stated previously that if ever there were a need for surgery, you would prefer it be done in your hospital so that the tissues may be saved for research. Also, would this operation be covered under any research grant?

On August 20, Barry was admitted to the Health Center at the University of Florida for surgery. Marge's mother cared for Sherry the week they were there; fortunately, both operations were covered by insurance. On August 22, while at Shands, Barry was given another psychological test which showed that his IQ of 88 at four years of age had within a two-year span dropped to 52. The clinical psychologist further wrote regarding behavioral observations:

Barry was not cooperative during the testing session, and praise and approval did not improve his performance. After the first few subtests it was necessary for his mother to come into the room for him to continue the testing. Mrs. Glider stated he had slept fitfully the night before and was most anxious to go home. As the tasks become more difficult, Barry rejected them or did the minimally accepted performance; i.e. placing the block in the frame with no attempt at problem solving.

The results of this examination places Barry at the lower limits of the mild retardation range with respect to mental functioning. It is felt that Barry's uncooperativeness was an adverse factor in the testing results. It was recommended to Mrs. Glider that she encourage Barry to play simple table games which involve both social interaction such as waiting his turn, following rules of the game, etc. and intellectual functions such as counting, problem solving, etc. Our findings are consistent with those of the educatable mentally retarded.

Simple games like clapping hands and singing were tried, but to no avail. It was like entertaining a small baby who enjoys the show but cannot participate. He couldn't even sing his favorite song, "Going bye-bye to somewhere…"

Denny's voice broke as he watched his son's decline. "He can't hit the ball anymore, Marge. He doesn't recognize the game. He's just a walking baby."

In the fall of 1969, Barry started elementary school for the trainable mentally retarded. As was always the case, Barry loved school and loved other children. Although he looked forward to attending class, he suddenly began to show strange behavior whenever Marge tried to take him to the bathroom. He became hysterical, grabbing the doorjamb and screaming in terror. Not knowing what to do, she mentioned this to the teacher's aide in Barry's classroom, a woman who also had an older retarded son. The teacher's aide bit her lip, then pulled Marge aside. "What I want to tell you must remain in confidence," she said in a low voice. Perplexed, Marge agreed. "Barry's teacher is locking Barry in the bathroom every time he wets his pants."

"What!" Marge cried in horror. "I can't believe anyone could be so cruel!" Finding it hard to catch her breath, she shook her head. Once her breathing was restored, she decided that she and Denny would have an immediate conference with the principal and everyone else involved. After a very heated conference, it was agreed that the teacher's aide would take care of Barry. Angry and vocal, Marge insisted, "The teacher is to have *nothing* whatsoever to do with Barry. She may have read all the right books about special education, but since Barry doesn't fit any of those chapters, she's been treating him inhumanly."

Despite being treated kindly by the aide, Barry was steadily growing less responsible and more uncontrollable. He had entered a phase of stomping toes for fun, including the toes of the aide who lost two toenails. Since Barry was still in corrective shoes, these stomps felt like they came from steel boots. He thought it was a game, just as he had thought it a game while at Shands when he had turned over a large stuffed chair with a young female resident sitting in it. Everyone was shocked by Barry's unbelievable strength.

It scared Marge to death to know that every moment Barry's brain deteriorated, his body grew stronger, as though one were compensating for the other. Barry had entered his own world. This heartless disease had stolen his brilliant mind while distorting his once coordinated body. Nothing was in sync. He could not remember the little boy he had been nor had no realization of the boy he was. Whether a blessing or a curse, he had no awareness of this cruel twist of fate.

He simply *was*.

Hoping against hope, it came as no surprise when at the end of the school year, they were told by Dekalb County that Barry did not fit into any of their programs. "We're permanently removing him from the school system."

Marge found herself begging. "Please, isn't there some other alternative? Barry loves this school. He needs to be around other children."

There was no trace of kindness in the answer given: "Your son doesn't belong here or in the public-school system. He is *not* educable or trainable. He cannot return. He does not fit anywhere."

Their lives would have been unbearable had it not been for the Pine Lake Baptist Church near their home. Their Sunday school teacher and his wife, Dr. John Brooks and Mary Jane—also their neighbors—were especially kind. "Whenever you have to go to Shands, I'll care for Sherry," Mary Jane offered. Although Sherry was a mama's girl, as well as mature for her age—a second mother who tried to help in any way she could as well as being a child who was practically raising herself—she responded to Mary Jane's love.

The more Barry declined, the more difficult it became to attend church. Like an Indian war dance chant, Barry began a piercing yell, which he felt compelled to employ during services. During one particular Sunday service, Barry was unusually loud in church.

"Barry's disturbing the family in front of us," Marge whispered to Denny.

Denny shook his head futilely as he tried to control Barry. Nothing worked. When the service ended, the family in front turned around to say something, but before they could, Marge apologized. "I know how angry you must be at him. I promise we'll not bring him back."

Their response shocked Marge and Denny. "We think it's wonderful you still bring him to church and come yourselves."

Not everyone felt that way. The answer to this problem came in the form of a sixty-year-old angel named Mrs. Deal. She had worked in the church nursery for over forty years and had raised several generations of church children. "I take care of the three-year-olds. Barry can stay with me. You need to have time to attend church rather than not attending. Church shouldn't be just for those physically well. That's not what Jesus was all about, was He?"

There were others who helped. One family, the Meltons, owned a plumbing business. Marge was quietly pulled aside and asked if money was needed to help Barry.

"No," Marge whispered as tears filled her eyes. "Money can't help Barry. If it could, we'd sell everything we had, but it can't."

Another angel arrived in the form of a church friend named Jo Cornwall. Marge's age, she had a little boy younger than Barry. "Marge," she offered, "if you have to take Sherry to the doctors or go to the store, anything, I'll take Barry."

"He's such a handful, Jo."

"I can handle him for a few hours. After all, since he can't attend school anymore, you have him twenty-four hours a day. You need a break now and then. In fact, I don't know *how* you do it."

Neither did she. She often felt that her breaking point was near. Tranquility and peace seemed a fragmented memory. Barry had become so destructive that she dare not keep anything on the tables— nothing could be in reach of his sweeping arms. When Denny was home, he tried as hard as possible to be patient with Barry's temper tantrums and destructive behavior, but he often, ashamedly, found himself exploding in rage at what Barry did.

Their home had become a war zone with Barry as their daily landmine. Each day was met with the awful question, *What next?*

Still, the greatest casualty of this raging war was a seven-year-old boy with no place to go and no place to grow.

*****

A mother's memory of her five-year-old son

"Mommy, guess what I finded out today?"

"What, Barry?"

"I finded out that if you hide your peas in your grandpa's iced tea, he'll find out."

13

Why Us, God?

Challenges make you discover things about yourself that
you never really knew. They're what make the instrument
stretch—what makes you go beyond the norm.

—Tyson

The truth that dawned on Marge was so painful that she was totally
unequipped to deal with it. Not only was Barry going to die, but
also it now seemed the life that remained would be denied dignity.
"Perhaps you and Mr. Glider should consider institutionalizing
Barry," was the only suggestion the public-school system offered.

"No one is going to take my child away!"

While Sherry started kindergarten, Barry, now eight, was forced
to remain home with her. Barry was dying. And in his dying, he was
already being denied "life."

There was no need to take him back to the Shands Research
program. He hated it as the tests were often painful. Hearing him
cry in another room was much too much to bear. Shands could not
help him nor save him. No one could. The most she could do was
make him as happy and as comfortable as possible. They would love
him and try to be patient with him. But they must also find time
for Sherry. She needed to be loved. With delayed reaction, Marge
suddenly wondered *when* and *how* baby Sherry had grown into this

adorable little five-year-old who, in becoming a second mother to Barry and friend to her, had grown far too mature for her age. She hoped that someday Sherry would not regret that her own childhood had been stolen while her brother's life was ebbing away. At this thought, Marge tried desperately to pray, but nothing spiritual claimed her. Instead she was standing in the middle of a solitary spiritual void where agony and terror reigned, where fatigue had drained her. No matter how she pleaded with God, comfort was not found. Not intending to, she found herself railing at God, shaking her fists and screaming, "Why? Why us, why Barry?"

She didn't know if Denny's being gone all week made the situation better or worse. No matter which way she turned, there were shades drawn between her and any further ray of hope. She had run out of even the will to *want* to believe. She was a robot doing mechanical things in a mechanical way. To *feel* meant to hurt, and she did not want to hurt anymore.

Day in and day out it was the two of them: Barry and her. His behavior had reached the point where she could no longer take him to a grocery store or shopping or even to church. Destruction and more destruction was the end result of his energy. Just going to the bathroom became a juggling act. It was growing worse by the minute, especially that evening while Barry and Sherry were seated at the kitchen table. Barry, totally out of control, was screaming and was breaking everything in reach. Denny, as usual, was out of town. Totally distraught, she was holding a Melmac plate. Without thinking, she aimed it at Barry. Suddenly, as though some invisible hand reached out to redirect her rage, she felt herself turn; and with extraordinary strength, she threw the plate violently against the kitchen wall. Despite Melmac being tough, it shattered into many pieces, the force and noise of its crash bringing terror to both children's eyes.

Falling to the floor in convulsive sobs, she was horrified that she could have hurt Barry, yet for one fleeting moment, she wondered about that *invisible hand!* Had it been real? Or was she simply going crazy? Oh, God! What was happening to her!

By the time Denny arrived home for the weekend, she felt too numb and too shamed to confess what had happened. How could she explain to anyone that she almost hurt her little boy, a little boy who was in pain and dying? What kind of a monster had she become?

Still disconnected from what she had done, she awoke wearily. It was Saturday morning, and Denny was asleep. Slowly she dressed and went into the dining room. As though in a trance, she pulled a chair away from the table and over to a corner where she sat, as if a child being punished, facing the wall.

Denny, hearing her heart-wrenching sobs, came to her. His face grew deeply disturbed. "Marge?" he asked cautiously. "What's wrong?"

The wife and mother named Marge Glider failed to respond in any way. She continued to stare at the corner walls. Marge had finally broken. She was undeniably in the throes of a mental breakdown. Life could no longer be faced, yet it could not be run from either.

At least not at that moment. At that moment, she was in some parenthesis—connected yet not truly "a part of."

Refusing to move or to respond to Denny, she wondered what they would do when she went insane? She even imagined their reactions, and when she did, she took a strange delight in thinking how everyone would be sorry. The strain had become too unbearable. She no longer cared if she lived or died.

The truth was, she didn't have the strength to care anymore. Or to even die. Like the walls she chose to face, she felt cornered with no way out.

"Marge, you've got to get some help," Denny begged. "I don't know what to do anymore. I know that you need my help, but I *have* to work now more than ever."

Her emotions were so numb that she felt invisible straps binding her. In a strange sense, it felt good to be going insane. Finally, after facing the wall for a long time, after realizing that true insanity had not totally taken hold, she agreed to see her doctor, who prescribed a huge bottle of Valium. She debated a week as to whether to use it but then decided that the last thing Barry needed was a mother who was a drug addict. What she did not tell anyone was that she did *not* trust herself not to consume the entire bottle. Flushing the pills down the toilet, she opted to seek out the advice of her church pastor, Reverend Wray Ivey.

"I'm locked in a prison with Barry." She admitted her strange and recent behavior. "If only there was a school for Barry, some respite that would free me for a few hours, something that would give me strength to face the rest of the day with him. As it is whenever I'm not trying to placate or entertain him, he's smashing things, hurting me, kicking me." She sobbed openly. "I'm at the end of my rope."

Reverend Ivey covered her hand with his. "Marge, you don't have to be strong twenty-four hours a day. You're human. And you're also very young. You and Denny have handled this amazingly well for such a young couple. Frankly, I'm astounded at how strong you've been." Pausing, he tilted his head. "How is Barry with Sherry?"

This one act of caring caused a stillness to settle over her. Her breathing returned to normal. "Barry's very good with Sherry. She's like a little mother to him, always has been. It's as if God—in His taking of Barry with the one hand—gave us Sherry with the other." Her eyes dropped for a moment as she thought of how dear Sherry was, how unwittingly this little angel had been pushed to the background. The moment she thought of the word *angel*, she also thought of Betty Jo and, in doing so, immediately felt God's presence; and when she did, she silently thanked Him for Sherry.

"Although I'm genuinely concerned about the state of your mind," Reverend Ivey said, "I'm also upset that Barry is being denied further education. He's not a throwaway—no child should be. I'm going to see what I can do."

"Can something be done?" she asked hopefully.

He nodded. "*Something has to be done*," he stressed. "And we're going to find that something."

Two weeks later, the search was over. The moment she saw Reverend Ivey at her front door, she sensed good news. "I've found an experimental school less than fifteen minutes from here. It's a new concept that's only two years old, a birth-to-death program for families who do not want their children institutionalized yet need help in maintaining them at home."

For the first time in months, Marge felt a ray of light enter the dark rooms of her mind. In a state of excited shock, she hit him with a thousand questions. Slowing her down, he explained that the school was called The DeKalb Training Center for the Profoundly Retarded. "The director is Mrs. Oreta Cook. I've heard she's an exceptional lady. The school runs five days a week from 8:30 a.m. to 2:30 p.m. and only closes for two weeks at Christmas. It's a year-round program because children like Barry cannot take a three-month summer break as they'd lose all of the progress made."

Marge quickly counted the hours between 8:30 a.m. and 2:30 p.m. "Six hours!" she cried out. Then in order to calm her beating heart, she drew back, ashamed that she was so grateful to have Barry gone for a while. "Will they take Barry?" she asked softly.

Reverend Ivey smiled. "Yes, Marge, I believe they will. I've made an appointment for you. From all I've learned, Barry will qualify. For six hours a day Barry will be a little boy going to school, and you'll be like any other mother, glad he's there, anxious to see him when he returns."

A series of tests by the DeKalb County Health Department for skill, comprehension, recognition, and general behavior were given to Barry, all of which he failed. "I know he can do better at these tests at another time," Marge defended, especially when told that Barry should have entered the program two years earlier. Marge suffered a feeling of being insulted. *Those* other children at the school were severely handicapped.

Barry was not *that* bad.

As she and Denny waited in the reception room for further instructions, they turned around in shock. Sitting there was Barry's twin! They could barely believe it. The other little boy and Barry, who were instantly drawn to each other, began playing together as if old friends. Somehow, they knew they spoke the same language, one perhaps that only the heart could hear.

Trying not to stare, Marge and Denny wanted to know if this little boy's parents resembled them? Strangely, as much as their sons appeared "twins," the parents were as different as night was from day, their common link being both boys suffered from Hurler syndrome.

The boys were immediately attracted to each other because they recognized a relationship that could be understood, and although their bond was unspoken, it was a *sharing* of two spirits on the most profound level. Both were angels with broken wings, but angels nonetheless.

Marge's second shock came when she saw that the training center was located *directly across* the street from the school DeKalb County had removed Barry from! Not once had the DeKalb County Board of Education mentioned the center or offered hope of any kind. Was it a case of not caring or simply a case of the right hand not knowing what the left hand was doing? Marge preferred to believe the latter while actually believed the former.

A third shock arrived when she saw the school itself: it was located in the old Hamilton High School building in Scottdale, one of the poorest slum areas in DeKalb County. It had been closed since the fifties due to integration. Now, rat and bug infested, it had been left to rot. The county owned the building, but since the program was federally funded by the Department of Human Resources, they would not repair it. "Why doesn't the federal government fix it up?" Marge questioned after having met Oreta Cook.

"The federal government won't spend the money because it doesn't own the building," Oreta replied.

"Then why doesn't the federal government buy the building?" Marge asked.

"They won't buy it because it's in such disrepair."

With that piece of governmental logic out of the way, Marge and Oreta laughed, and in their laughter, a new friendship was born.

Oreta Cook, an attractive slim blond in her late forties, was elegant, articulate, and extremely intelligent. Despite shunning the spotlight in order to focus attention on others, everyone *knew* she was the energy behind the light. No matter how well-dressed, she never hesitated to get down on the floor on her hands and knees to finger paint or hug a child. Undemanding, she nonetheless expected every student be treated with love and dignity.

"What did you do before you took over this school?" Marge asked as Oreta took her on a tour.

"I was a special ed teacher. I've always loved children. Plus my husband is very supportive of what I'm doing. He has to be. Everyone has my home telephone number, which means I'm on-call twenty-four hours a day. I've a grown son and daughter, and although they're normal, I've always related to children like Barry. They're *very* special."

"Special?" Marge asked.

"Yes. They're not only a challenge to themselves but to all of us who care. These children make us reach deep inside—to take that extra step in not only giving them love but in finding a solution to their problems."

Marge felt smaller in Oreta's presence.

Knowing how Marge felt, Oreta continued. "Marge, you're carrying the bulk of Barry's problems. It's okay to feel frustrated. You're doing a good job. He's your son and a part of your heart. You're a wonderful mother."

For the first time in a long time, Marge felt as if she counted, that she wasn't sitting on the sidelines after all.

The guided tour displayed a building with no air-conditioning; holes in the roof; puddles in the hall from a recent rain; heating that only worked on occasion; and windows that were cracked, broken, and boarded up. "From the many break-ins," Oreta explained, shaking her head.

Despite her dismay over the condition of the school, Marge's humor surfaced. "Well, since there's not much for thieves to take, maybe we should set out a plate for them to leave donations."

The aged school consisted of offices, a gym, kitchen, and various classrooms with a staff of approximately thirty. Even though there were only about five students per classroom, each teacher had an aide in order that individual attention and training be given. In the back of the school was a fenced-in play area that actually had grass—the result of a caring staff and caring parents. Distressed by the condition of the school, Marge willed herself to see beyond its external: internally the school held the type of spirit and love rarely found. There was truth in not judging a book by its cover.

Hope had been restored.

Marge learned that the focus of the school was to offer each student and their family the most encouraging support and training humanly possible. The program was based upon giving each student individual education and care by first evaluating where they were physically, mentally, and emotionally and where they needed to go. This training/learning process embraced such elements as toilet training, feeding, dressing, and in some instances, just learning to hold one's head up. "We have one little girl who couldn't walk," Oreta explained. "Even the doctors had given up on her. We taught her to walk. You can't imagine the emotions we experienced when she took her first step."

"I think I can," Marge whispered, while thinking that with every step taken with Oreta, she, too, was learning to move forward. It was easy to see that Oreta gave her life to this school, as did the other teachers. Obviously, there was unbelievable support among this rare and beautiful team who sang forth a tune established by Oreta: *If you couldn't love all of these kids and adults exactly as they were, you weren't welcome.* Those teachers without this attitude were not hired, or if by chance they had slipped through the system, their stay was short-lived.

As they walked to the various classes, Oreta told Marge that the enrollment exceeded a hundred students. "It's equally divided between Black and White students and covers all economic levels. The only requirement of this school is that *your* child *needs* us."

Marge felt her bitterness fading. People no longer cringed when they saw her with Barry but instead greeted them with sincere smiles, warm hugs, and an overpowering loving spirit. Suddenly Barry broke loose as he saw the little boy who looked like his twin. Marge smiled in recognition of his parents, and in that smile, yet another friendship was born.

Assigned the same class, a Black lady named Ms. Shropshire was waiting for them at the classroom door. Bubbling and smiling widely, she held out her arms for Barry to come to her for a big hug, which he gladly gave. Children it seemed, no matter what level of their existence, responded to love.

Leaving Barry to scoot into the classroom with his new friends, Marge glanced at Oreta and saw a familiar look in her eyes. It reminded her of someone, *someone very special.*

*****

A mother's memory of her five-year-old son

"MOMMY, GUESS WHAT I FINDED OUT TODAY?"

"What, Barry?"

"I FINDED OUT THAT IF YOU KICK SOME KID IN THE KNEE WITH BOTH FEET AT THE SAME TIME, YOU'LL FALL DOWN."

14

Going Bye-Bye

I had to set limits to knowledge in order to make place for faith.

—E. Kant

Although it appeared to Marge that God had personally created a welcoming center for Barry, the outside world still shunned him. As the doctors predicted, Barry's physical appearance was changing as his mind deteriorated. His once perfect little body took on a skeletal deformity as each organ, disturbed by some abnormality of the body chemistry, became enlarged and out of proportion. Barry had become a precious little boy with a fatal disease.

Her precious son, although growing more deformed with each passing day, was not grotesque. He was a little boy who wanted to play with the neighborhood children but was, for the most, part shunned.

Standing to the side of the yard, he would longingly watch the other children bat balls, play tag, and laugh together. Sometimes he would walk *through* their games, but he was no longer a *part* of them. Sensing his presence disturbed them, he preferred to stay close to the house, except for one Sunday afternoon.

Keeping watch over Barry, Marge had turned away from the kitchen window for a few minutes. When she looked back, Barry was gone. She shouted for Denny. "Barry's disappeared!"

While Denny combed the neighborhood, Marge called the neighbors. No one had seen Barry. Within a matter of minutes, most of the neighbors had joined the search. Still not finding Barry, Marge yelled that she was going to call the police. Before she had time to dial the telephone, Denny happened to walk by their car. Sitting on the floor of the passenger's side was Barry who was happily pulling tape from a car cassette, oblivious to the panic surrounding him.

"I feel so embarrassed," Marge told Denny. "I've apologized to everyone who looked for Barry."

"It's okay, Marge," Denny soothed. "Other little boys do what Barry did—get into trouble—and cause their parents to lose hair or grow some gray ones. The positive is that this demonstrates how lucky we are to live in a neighborhood that cares."

In that sense, Denny was right. But in the sense that Barry was a lonely little boy still saddened her. When the doorbell rang, she was still thinking how she could get Barry to be more accepted, to join in games without destruction. Opening the door, a stranger eyed her.

"I'm a social worker from DeKalb County," he announced. Had there not been compassion in his voice, Marge may have suffered alarm. "Some of your neighbors have reported Barry to us," the man explained.

Instant fear took hold. "What? But *why?*"

With obvious discomfort, the man drew a few steps back. "They believe Barry's dangerous." He paused, then lowered his voice. "They're afraid he might harm their children."

There were no words to describe what she felt. It went beyond hurt, anger, even shock. It was if she had been struck down by an all-consuming, invisible disease. This was *not* the Middle Ages where people were so heartless as to believe sick children were demon-possessed! Dear God! Surely humanity had outgrown such a horrible indictment! How could *anyone* think this ill little boy would be capable of harming anyone! Finding her voice, Marge stared at the man. "Barry's *only* eight years old."

"I know, Mrs. Glider," the man replied gently. "Complaints like these are always blown out of proportion. It seems that Barry has been ringing a neighbor's doorbell. That incident apparently was the springboard for this accusation."

"Nobody has complained to us about Barry ringing doorbells," Marge stammered. "And even if he's doing that, how can that lead anyone to believe he'd harm other children? I don't understand."

This isn't the Middle Ages, again plagued her mind. Or was it? she added, thinking that perhaps history *did* keep repeating itself over and over again.

The man sighed. "If I were you, I wouldn't make this an 'us against them' neighborhood war. You folks have to live here, Barry lives here. Sometimes it only takes one or two people to turn a molehill into a mountain."

Too proud to allow this caring stranger to see she was on the brink of crying, she fought back tears. "Why would anyone want to do this to us? We have so many problems as it is."

"Malice, that sort of rubbish."

"Malice equates to hatred. *Who* in God's name hates us that much?"

The man scratched his head. "Sometimes a clue rests with someone you know. I've found it's not always strangers hating strangers. It could be closer to home than that."

Marge shook her head in protest. "The people we're close to are good people, religious people."

"Maybe, but I've learned that sometimes folks have just enough religion to make them know how to hate but not enough to make them know how to love."

Barry was kept in the house for the next two weeks until Sears was able to put a chain-link fence around the backyard. Totally isolated and imprisoned from neighborhood contact, Barry looked at her as though she had mortally wounded him or, to be exact, had imprisoned him.

How could she explain to this bewildered, terminally ill little boy that by his deterioration, mass hysteria and fear had erupted, and as in the Middle Ages, the *good people* wanted him destroyed or at the very least, locked up and *out of sight.* All the while she dealt with Barry's second death sentence, she quietly searched for the person behind such a foundless, cruel rumor. She had always felt that she lived in a close-knit neighborhood where people helped each other, not harmed each other.

By accident, another neighbor confessed that a secret petition had circulated in regards to Barry. Once again, Marge reacted with shock. "A petition? What was it about?"

"It asked that we sign our names requiring that Barry be locked up in an institution. Except for one other family and the people who originated it, everyone in the neighborhood refused to sign it."

Outrage smothered her shock. "I can't believe this! It's so underhanded!"

"It's just a piece of worthless paper, Marge," her neighbor said kindly. "Stupid and vicious."

"No, it's not! This is more than a stupid, silly piece of paper. It's evil! It's a monstrosity." Suddenly she turned and looked out the window at Barry. He was standing alone staring through the chain-link fence at children he could no longer play with. She turned back to her neighbor. "The one family who signed the petition, who are they?"

There was a brief pause. "Marge, I don't want to start anything. Still, I have to put myself in your shoes. The people who signed it are the Timms."

"Our next-door neighbors? Why would they sign such a petition? They know us, know Barry. Their children are Sherry's best friends. I can't believe this!" She paused, then asked, "*Who* is the family who originated the petition?"

Another pause ensued. "I'd rather not be the one to tell you. Believe me, what they've put out has come back to them tenfold. Hardly anyone bothers with them. If they could do this to you, then who knows what they're capable of doing to any of us? Believe me when I say if tar-and-feathering were legal, these people would have been tar and feathered long ago. Knowing who they are would further hurt you. You've suffered enough. The reason no one wanted you and Denny to know was to protect you. The Timms were pawns. Forget about this. Instead remember we all love you and are here for you."

Left with the burden of anger, Marge tried to remain calm, tried to remind herself that starting a war would do no one any good. She felt trapped in her desire for peace versus her desire for confrontation. No matter how hard she tried, the awfulness of what had happened would not leave her. Where ever she went, whoever she saw, she wondered, Is this my Judas? She detested the fact that this growing hatred was eating at her like a multiplying cancer. Almost ill from what was occurring, she told Denny she was going to Sunday-evening church service.

"You rarely attend evening services?" he questioned.

"I need to go, Denny. And I need to go alone. If I don't go right now, I don't think I'll remain healthy."

During a sermon she could not listen to, every breath she took was like a prayer. She asked for peace, guidance, and, above all, understanding. Suddenly a voice told her what she must do. The words in her mind were *not* her words nor her thoughts but were strong enough to cause her to immediately leave the church and drive directly to the Timms. She thought about the voice and then thought about Betty Jo. Somehow the two images connected.

Without fear, she rang the Timms's doorbell. June Timms stared at her with surprise.

"May I come in?" Marge asked, grateful there was no anger in her voice.

"Please do," June stammered. "We've wanted to call you but didn't know what to say."

"Then you know why I'm here?"

"Yes, please come in."

Once inside, Marge apologized for Barry's behavior. "I'm sorry that Barry was ringing your doorbell. It had to be irritating. Had I been aware of this, I would have put a stop to it immediately. We have a problem with Barry, as you know. I'm sorry it became your problem."

June began to cry. "Marge, we're so ashamed. You may not believe this, but our actions have hurt us more than they've hurt you. We've wanted to call you so many times but were afraid to. We knew immediately how wrong we had been, how stupid we were to be so easily led. We never said or even thought Barry was trying to harm our children. I just couldn't take the constant doorbell ringing. That's no excuse of course—"

"No, it's not," Marge replied softly.

"We know your family has suffered so much, and we're so sorry to have added to that suffering."

The energy of being spiritually guided precluded any need for revenge. She hugged and forgave June, then asked, "Will you please do one favor for me?"

Wiping the tears from her eyes, June nodded. "Of course, anything."

"Tell me *who* was behind the petition."

June glanced at her husband nervously. He nodded. "Tell her, June. She needs to know the truth."

June nodded in return, then looking at Marge, said. "It was Roy and Sandy Wilson."

The depth of such betrayal disturbed Denny as well, although he did not want to dwell on it. On the other hand, Marge felt the need for revenge with incredible regularity. Once more, a sense of overwhelming hatred was all-consuming and was so destructive that she didn't even want to pray to God for peace. It was as if in the savoring of hatred satisfaction might be found.

"Honey," Denny interjected, his eyes showing the depth of his hurt, "using your energies to hate Roy and Sandy is self-destructive. You have to care about someone to hate them, and they're not worth caring about. Remember, they have to look at themselves in the mirror, but so do you. Do you want to look at the face of hatred or the face of forgiveness?"

Marge walked over to Denny and leaned into him. "Should I forgive them?" she whispered. "But how can I? Denny, they've been our friends since Florida. Roy lived with us the entire time he hunted for a home for his family. We not only opened our home to him, to Sandy and their children, but we gave them our hearts and our trust."

"God forgives."

In truth, she was too tired not to forgive. "All right," she replied, then thought, *I didn't ask God to give me peace this time, but He answered me anyway through Denny.*

The DeKalb Training Center, having openly and warmly embraced Barry, welcomed Marge into their parent volunteering program. As deep friendships formed between Marge and the staff, Barry couldn't wait for each day to arrive in order to go to a school where he was accepted and loved. There were children better off than Barry but also children far worse, which helped bring balance to Marge's perspective.

Added to the day-to-day surveillance of Barry's decline was the desire to give Sherry the attention she deserved. "I need to take Sherry places," Marge lamented, "but finding a babysitter for Barry is almost impossible."

Occasionally they were able to hire teenagers from the church or the daughter of a close friend to sit, but this did not occur with regularity. Recently disaster struck upon hiring a new sitter. Right after she and Denny had left to see a movie, Barry had thrown up.

This was followed by diarrhea that soiled the large easy chair Barry had been sitting in. The sitter had cleaned up Barry and put him to bed but had refused to clean the chair. When they returned, they were not only greeted by the remaining mess but by a house permeated by stench. Fortunately, with Barry now in the center, some hours were found for herself. When Barry was home, her work was at an all-time high. All previous potty training for Barry had long disappeared. "I have to change his clothes at least eight to ten times a day. Feeding him is like feeding a wild animal," Marge cried. "He runs and screams in those high-pitched squeals and tears up everything in the house. I can't keep anything in reach—no books, no knick-knacks, no flower arrangements. Sometimes I think I'll go insane."

What she could not tell Denny or anyone was that suicide had lately become a part of her troubled thinking. The only thing that stopped her was leaving Barry's condition to others. Even Denny found Barry impossible to handle. She was too afraid to end her life for fear that Barry would be institutionalized for what remained of his life. The irony of this rationalization struck deep.

Knowing the depth of her despair, her parents had moved from Florida in order to take Barry every weekend. "At least for forty-eight hours, you can give Sherry a normal family life," her mother offered.

"I wish I could enjoy those weekends," Marge admitted. "I feel so guilty even *wanting* to enjoy time away from Barry."

Her mother's counsel was always colored with loving patience. "Marge, you're trying to be superhuman. Wanting time away from Barry isn't a sign of weakness but of survival. Sherry deserves her due. She needs time to be a child. She's only a little girl, and although she's been a real trooper in protecting Barry, she *needs* her mommy and daddy too. We love Barry. We love all of you. We want to help. Taking Barry is the relief you need and deserve. Besides, Barry loves being with us." Her voice drifted off. "Remember, too, that these moments with Barry are precious to us, moments we won't have forever."

Barry grew sicker and sicker with congestion, cough, and a fever, which now hit every few weeks until it never left. He was allergic to dampness, and if outside after six in the evening, he was always sick the following day. All sorts of medicines were prescribed. Eventually nothing worked. "No one wants Barry to suffer," the doctors told her, "but there's nothing more we can do."

Hearing such finality, Marge made every effort to pull herself together. She had long known the truth, but hearing it from the medical community held its own level of shock. Barry could not last much longer. His stomach had become very large, his lips had increased in size, and he drooled constantly. At nights he was unable to sleep because breathing was a gasping torture. At first they propped him up on double pillows, but after finding him wandering around in the middle of the night like a lost baby, Marge sat up every night holding him in her arms in an attempt to make his breathing easier. There was so much fear in his innocent eyes, but since all language had disappeared, it was impossible for him to tell them where it hurt. He could not understand what was happening to him. His arms and legs were almost immovable as his joints ceased to work, almost as if they were truly encased in stone.

Barry's body was dying by degrees.

One morning at three o'clock, Marge, exhausted, began to cry openly as she held Barry. He was choking for breath, each breath more painful than the preceding. Hearing her cries, Denny ran into Barry's bedroom. He was also filled with fear and helplessness. "Marge?"

"Barry's suffocating, Denny. He's suffocating. It would be better if God took Barry now. I love him too much to see him suffer like this. And I hate God for allowing this. I *hate* Him!"

"It's all right, Marge. God knows the truth, knows *why* you're crying. It's all right, it's all right…," he soothed.

But it wasn't all right. Time had run out. All hopes for a cure or a miracle had been crushed. They had to face the truth that Barry's young life was drawing to a close, at least on the physical level.

"Denny, I don't want to withdraw from God," Marge sobbed. "But instead of a ray of light, God's more of a filmy image—gauzy and gray." She was saddened that God no longer fit her image of a caring Father but was instead a dim and distant stranger Who she had only slightly known or perhaps had never known. Since she perceived God as having abandoned her, she found it impossible to remain faithful. And, in her lack of faith, felt even more abandoned.

As Barry neared his tenth birthday, his continuing deterioration kept him home more and more from the training center. In order to give substance and direction to the paths they were forced to travel, she wrote down her thoughts:

> *I live in constant fear that he will die,*
> *The Lord will take him—don't know why.*
> *I only know that he must go,*
> *Even though I love him so.*

Awaiting the arrival of her parents to take Barry for his birthday weekend visit, Marge sat in the kitchen playing horsey and patty cake with him. She almost told him about the new red tricycle hidden for him at his grandparents' house. It was an early birthday gift planned for that afternoon. For a strange reason, Barry appeared calm, and his laughter filled the house with happiness. At that moment, he was neither sick nor retarded but was instead a normal little boy having fun. Marge thought, *This is a precious memory to store for the future.*

Early Sunday morning, when the telephone rang, Marge and Denny came to their feet.

"It's Barry," Marge's mother cried. "He's very sick. He's been up all night and has literally chewed the wooden sill of the window near his bed. You've got to come over right now!"

Premonition and fear kept Marge and Denny from speaking to each other during the drive to her parents' house. The *unspeakable* made them exiles from each other. Their eyes never wavered from fear, while a cold bleakness and resignation made them stare straight ahead. By the time they arrived, Marge's mother had Barry dressed and was waiting. There was a desperation and fear in her eyes that mirrored theirs.

Barry gave a little shout of glee as his grandmother sat him on the trunk of their car in order to open the car door. "He had a snack earlier, a Twinkie," her mother murmured more to herself than to Marge. "It's his favorite treat."

Suddenly Barry offered up his arms and gave his grandmother a large hug. She stepped into his embrace and kissed him on each cheek, then looked at Marge with an expression never seen before.

It was both peaceful and comforting.

Marge's face was filled with curiosity. For a moment, she remained where she was standing, then reached for Barry and put him in the back seat. His fingers touched her gently, as though patting her, as though saying, "It's okay, Mommy. Boo-boo fixed."

As they pulled out of the driveway, Barry turned and got on his hands and knees. Looking out the rear window of the car, he waved his hand, and for the first time in a very long time sang, "Going bye-bye to somewhere—to somewhere…"

*****

A mother's memory of her five-year-old son

"MOMMY, GUESS WHAT I FINDED OUT TODAY?"

"What, Barry?"

"I FINDED OUT THAT YOU DON'T ALWAYS HAVE TO SMACK A BASE-BALL FOR A DADDY TO SAY YOU DONE GOOD."

15

He Is with Me

If the work of God could be comprehended by
reason, it would be no longer wonderful, and faith
would have no merit if reason provided proof.

—Pope Gregory

"I've called the doctor," Marge told Denny once they were home.
"He's phoned in a prescription that might help Barry with his breathing. I'll take Sherry with me to the drugstore."

Denny drew close to Barry and patted him on the head. "Barry
and I can watch the Falcons play, right, son?"

Barry, as though seeming to understand what he had not earlier
understood, nodded.

By the time Marge returned to the house, she could hear Denny
shouting. "The Falcons must have scored," she told Sherry. Walking
into the kitchen, her heart froze. Denny was not seated in front of the
television but was screaming into the telephone. Barry, with blood
running from his little mouth, was lying motionless on the kitchen
floor.

Marge fell to the floor screaming. Instinctively she knew that
nothing in her voice could arouse Barry. He was asleep forever.
Denny, still struggling to understand, shouted for the rescue squad
to come immediately.

Knowing God had taken Barry but still unable to accept what had happened, Marge rose and, crying, rushed blindly out the front door. A doctor lived five doors away and had always told her to call him at any time. With her world exploding, she felt as if she were running in slow motion. Not even the loss of one shoe interrupted her hazy yet frantic race. It seemed forever before she reached the doctor's house and hours more before he followed her back to Barry.

He, too, was visibly shaken as he examined the little boy lying on the kitchen floor. An interminable length of time passed before the doctor looked at them. Shaking his head said, "I'm sorry, *Barry's gone...*"

Time and space froze. Neither she nor Denny held a clear realization of events. It was as if they were standing on the fringes of a nightmare trying frantically to run from the images surrounding them. Internally screaming to awake, they knew an "awakening" was impossible.

The unthinkable had arrived.

Denny finally reacted, but Marge, now in total shock and denial, existed in a state of solitary confinement. She was trying to survive in a world now empty of a little boy's sounds, a world where her heart and soul were forever locked behind a steel door. Even the paramedics arrival occurred in a haze.

Knowing he must be strong, Denny took charge by supportively holding Marge and Sherry. "Would you take Sherry home with you?" he asked a neighbor family who had followed the rescue squad to their home.

Seven-year-old Sherry protested. "Daddy, no! I want to stay here with you and Mommy." Looking around the house, which was slowly filling with neighbor after neighbor, Sherry's large blue eyes filled with tears. "Where's Barry? *Where has be gone?*"

Denny uttered a muffled sob as he bent and tried to explain to Sherry the loss of her brother. How could he tell her that she would never see Barry again, at least not on earth? Scanning the house, he noted that Marge had been led to the den and was sitting on the couch. He had to go to her, but first, he had to be certain Sherry was being cared for.

"Sherry," a neighbor offered kindly, "why don't you come home with us so that your mommy and daddy can take care of things. Maybe you'd like some ice cream? We have some at our house."

"No," Sherry replied stubbornly. "I don't want any ice cream. I want to stay here." She turned to look at where her mother was sitting, then back at Denny. "*Where* is Barry, Daddy?"

Denny, still kneeling, shook his head, unable to speak.

Sherry reached out and gently touched his cheek. "We'll see Barry again, Daddy," she proclaimed with the strength of someone much older and wiser than he. "And he can see us too."

Marge stared down into the open coffin, which was surrounded by a circle of color that seemed more like a rainbow than flowers. What surprised her was how peaceful Barry looked. And even though her heart was crushed at seeing her baby so quiet, she was grateful that his suffering had ended.

He was innocent and new again.

The breath of life had left him, but his energy was still felt. He was still that precious little boy who loved to ride horses, play cowboys, hit a baseball to his dad, and ride a red tricycle with energy and zest. He was all that he had ever been, *yet more than he had ever been. He was whole.*

Her angel with broken wings had been called home.

"Bye-bye, my precious," she whispered. "You've gone somewhere—somewhere…"

Despite the huge double room filled with family and friends, so many that they spilled over into the long hallway of the funeral home, Marge couldn't keep her eyes off Barry. Silly things crossed her mind such as the fact Barry wasn't wearing one of his favorite outfits. Since he had died on a Sunday afternoon and since Monday was always laundry day, his best clothes were in the hamper. Because she had not been consciously aware enough to ask someone to wash Barry's clothes, he had been buried in sport shirt and slacks that were her least favorite. Wonderfully though, he held a rubber neon—and Band-Aided—Goofy in his hands. Sherry had given him Goofy, and it was one of his most prized toys, a toy she had chosen to place in her little brother's stilled hands.

Denny came to stand beside her. With his arm around her, she had forgotten how strong he could be. He and his father had taken care of the funeral arrangements, greeted the scores of people who came to their home laden with food and consolations, while at the same time he had led her from one numb reaction to another.

"Everyone from the church, the neighborhood, and the training center are here," Denny said as he inhaled deeply. "God has sent so many people to help us."

Remaining silent, Marge frowned. How could she tell Denny that earlier that morning, she had cursed God, that God had not received a reprieve or a blessing from her. She had decided that even though God had taken Barry, He had also allowed her baby years of suffering. Earlier that morning, she was tired of God, tired of praying to Him, tired of having begged Him to help Barry. God had *not* listened. That being the case, she had vowed to never again talk to God nor turn to Him. Barry was free of pain, but she was not. Her entire being had ached as if pierced by hot arrows. She could barely draw a breath without feeling torture. There was no way she could thank God for this.

Until something happened to interrupt her outburst.

Her mind returned to earlier that morning: with the house already filled with people, she had awakened feeling void of all feeling. Lying back in her bed, she had stared at the ceiling, wishing herself to die. How could she go on without Barry? Denny was a young man of thirty-three, and Sherry just a child of seven. They could start a new life without her. They were both lovable and could go forward, while her existence would keep them from living. Her life might force them to drown in her dark sea of depression. Logically, she knew that she would not die, but she also pledged never to leave her bed again. Her life was over. Praying to die, she felt the sun's rays coming in through the window. She had fought its warmth but was helpless to fight what next occurred:

The sun's warmth from the windows began to slowly move down her body from her head to her feet. It was the most wonderful, loving feeling of her life. It was nothing like she had ever experienced; it was so incredible! God was refilling her soul and returning her to life. Suddenly, it felt as if a branding iron had been placed on her forehead and with it the words, *He is with Me.*

Instantly she realized that although she had abandoned God, God had not abandoned her. While God had welcomed Barry back home, He was restoring her life by returning to her the *will* to live.

Arising from her bed, she bathed, then put on her favorite green dress for Barry's funeral. Before she left her bedroom, she turned and looked at the sunrays. In them she caught sight of the specks of dust that Barry often tried to catch, and for the briefest of moments, she saw Barry leaping and jumping about, saying, "I catching the sun, Mommy…"

Standing at the coffin, she continued to remember the words spoken earlier, *He is with Me.*

Her "once upon a time" now became "once upon a miracle." Renewed by a life force that would be impossible to explain, she looked up at Denny. "Where's Sherry?" she asked in the barest of whispers.

"She's sitting with your parents."

As friend after friend passed by the coffin and hugged her, a feeling of incredible peace set in. *Someone* else besides God was also with her, protecting her, gently leading her out of her tunnel of darkness. Her search for *who* that *someone* might be was interrupted when one of her neighbors pressed into her hand a copy of the Serenity Prayer: *"God, grant me the serenity to accept the things I cannot change, courage to change those things I can, and wisdom to know the difference."*

The courage to change those things I can embedded itself in her mind, and when it did, she once again heard the voice of Betty Jo, who also stressed, *Have the courage to change those things you can.* Without questioning *what* had occurred, she knew that there was much she had to do, but first she would ask everyone to leave the room, including Denny and Sherry. "I need to have a few minutes alone with Barry one last time," she told Denny. "You were the first to see him. I need to be the last."

Once alone she touched Barry's cheek. "I love you, Barry," she whispered. "Your daddy loves you, your sister and your grandparents love you. So many people love you and will miss you so much. You touched the hearts of everyone who met you. You're with God now, and you're happy and healthy again. You lived here like an angel with broken wings, but your wings are whole again, and you're soaring high with God. I'll see you again, my precious baby, sometime, *somewhere*."

As they drove to the cemetery, Marge looked out the rear window of the car. As far back as the eye could see, the many hills of Dekalb County were dotted by one car after another. It was both magnificent and unbelievable—a unity of strength that went beyond explanation. Yet it was not enough to prepare her for a final goodbye at Barry's gravesite. "I can't bear to leave him here," Marge cried hysterically as she knelt upon the naked earth. "Please, Denny, don't make me leave my baby here…"

Denny's strength drew her to her feet and close to him. "Honey, you're not leaving Barry here. This isn't *our* Barry anymore. He's with God. But he's also with us now, and he's looking down upon us. Think of Barry's love for you, how in his love he doesn't want you to suffer, just as you didn't want him to suffer. Love Barry enough to free him."

Somewhere in her despair, light was seeping through. Saying goodbye, even if only a temporary goodbye, was difficult. She had no idea how she would learn to live in a world without Barry.

Saying goodbye was so overwhelming that it temporarily blocked out the miracles that had and were taking place.

Back at the house, Marge broke away from the crowd in order to go into Barry's bedroom. He was still there, every animated inch of him. His scent and presence filled the air. From his bedside drawer, she drew out a faded piece of paper—another poem she had written titled simply BARRY.

> The smile remains but the sparkle is gone,
> The laughter now has a ring of its own.
> The body built so strong and fair,
> Is now gnarled and changed—
> It's just not there.
> The brain is damaged so they say,

The promised life is taken away.
Lord, help me to be strong—
The child I wanted was not for long.

Seesawing between despair and peace, Marge heard someone say, *How lucky you were to have had Barry. You had the rare opportunity to see life through the eyes of a beautiful little retarded child. God was generous and wise when He sent you Barry, and you were lucky to have had him.*

Marge looked around. She was completely alone, yet she was not alone. Suddenly, for only an instant, she felt the words of Betty Jo.

*****

A mother's memory of her five-year-old son

"MOMMY, GUESS WHAT I FINDED OUT TODAY?"

"What, Barry?"

"I FINDED OUT THAT COVERING YOUR PEAS WITH KETCHUP MAKES 'EM TASTE BETTER."

16

Beyond the Shadows

Every human being has a responsibility for
injustice anywhere in the community.

—Scott Buchanan

Learning to live without Barry was more difficult than ever imagined. After having seen the face of Betty Jo, Marge was led to Barry's baby book. Secured inside was Betty Jo's gift: the silver dollar with the words *In God We Trust*.

"*How* did *you* know?" she questioned. "Were *you* preparing me for this?"

The road back to God was paved with difficulty. As much as she tried renewing her faith, a great deal of confusion lingered. She wanted desperately to allow God's hand to continue to lead her from her tunnel of darkness, yet she still suffered the feeling that her season of living in the sun was over. She was groping her way through a wilderness of such sadness that she wondered if she would ever find the pathway to light.

The simplest chores were bathed in a sea of emotional spasms. Even returning to the grocery store was traumatic. Automatically, she found herself reaching for some of Barry's favorite foods. This particular day, she began to sob so hard that she ran from the store, her tears so blinding that she questioned how she would find her way home. No one had warned her about doing things for the first time *without* Barry.

At home she was reminded that Barry was still there. Despite Kay having packed up his clothes, his bedroom was exactly as it had been, except Barry *wasn't* there.

Sherry walked in the room and looked around. "Mommy, Barry's in heaven, right?" Marge nodded.

"And he can see us, right?"

"I believe he can."

"Then why can't we see him?"

Marge smiled as she studied a child too wise for her age. Kneeling, Marge responded softly, "We can see Barry with our hearts because that's where our love is."

"Will God give him a bath like I did?"

In her laughter, she hoped that eventually the pain would lessen so that joy would be a part of her life rather than a rare moment. It was still so hard to see other parents with their sons and not ask, *Why our son? Why did Barry have to suffer so? Why couldn't we see him grow?*

Trying to meet the next day head-on was an effort that Denny understood but one which perplexed Sherry. Like all children, her faith was clear and binding. "Mommy," Sherry asked as she made her own peanut butter and jelly sandwich, "don't you love me anymore?"

Marge closed her eyes as she considered what to say to this wonderful little girl who had been too strong for so long. Opening her eyes, she walked to where Sherry stood and gently took the butter knife from her and began spreading the peanut butter for her daughter. For a split second, she was reminded that it was safe to have knives around. Finished making the sandwich, she kneeled before Sherry and touched her cheek. How beautiful this child was. The same God who had taken Barry had also given Sherry. "I love you very, very much, Sherry. I'm sorry you had to ask that question. When God took Barry home, I forgot that while He temporarily closed one door, He also opened up another."

Sherry turned to look at the closed kitchen door.

Marge again laughed. "What I meant is that God gave you to us. You are a gift from God."

Sherry tilted her head in question.

"I guess a lot of this doesn't make sense to you now, but someday I'll explain."

Sherry smiled. "I already know. I know God sent me here to be born so you wouldn't be lonely."

Marge smiled. "And to eat peanut butter and jelly sandwiches?"

Before stuffing her mouth with the mushy mixture, Sherry giggled. "I think God has peanut butter and jelly sandwiches in heaven 'cause what else would He feed His kids?"

It was time to absorb her loss and go on, but where? Where were those doors that would lead her away from the painful memories while at the same time keeping the happy memories?

"I want to be grateful to God for giving us Barry," Marge told Denny. "It hurts to even remember the happy times."

"I know," Denny consoled. He, too, was drawn into the past, and although he took relief in knowing Barry's suffering had ended, he also questioned *why* God had sent Barry to them? His faith dictated that nothing is for naught, that in time God would reveal to them the purpose of Barry's short life. It was still difficult to believe he would not see Barry again, nor toss him a ball. "I wish I could take back every spanking I ever gave Barry, every negative word spoken. I wish I had hugged him more. I have to live with that and it's not easy."

There was so much that had to be worked through. Perhaps they had expected there would be no backlash. She was ashamed now that she had actually taken satisfaction in once seeing Denny's guilt and pain, that she had warned him he'd feel this way. Now she knew that he had undertaken the heavy burden of being a young man who had to financially care for a wife and two children—one with a life-threatening disease. Not once had he shirked this duty.

The time had come to throw out the bathwater and keep the baby. After all, he was human. She was human. Life in itself was a mixture of balancing strengths with weaknesses, or as she had once been told, *"It takes both the rain and the sun to make a rainbow."*

It was time to move forward, time to *take on the courage to change those things that she could*—the training center.

Before Barry's death, she had been elected president of the center's parent group. There were many months left to serve should she wish. She decided that finishing out her term while helping other children at the school was something she could do with expertise. Plus, the training center had given Barry his last two years of happiness. Their love and acceptance had made her and Denny feel human again. It was a debt too huge to repay, but serving was a good way to start. She also was involved in Sherry's school. She quickly learned that, despite Sherry's maturity, Barry's death had affected her grades. Suddenly Marge was forced to focus upon another child, another school.

The contrast was both shocking and comforting.

Sherry's school was outstanding in every way. Beyond being brand-new, it was supported by parents and the community. Every other year, it won Georgia School of the Year. "It would win every year if allowed," Marge told Denny. "It's hard to believe that Barry's school is only five miles away from Sherry's. The training center is in the worst section of DeKalb County and in such deplorable condition that the fire marshal gave us an ultimatum: bring it up to standards or it will be closed."

"*Closed?*"

Catching her breath, Marge shook her head helplessly. "What will these children do *without* the center?"

"They can't continue to attend a school that's a fire hazard," Denny reminded. "Aren't there any funds anywhere to repair the center so that it meets state regulations?"

"Oreta has continually looked for help, but because the program is federal and the building is county, both sides say they can't do anything."

"This seems like an excuse *not* to help."

Marge sighed. "It is. There's an army of red tape obstructing us."

Denny rubbed his chin.

"Denny?" Marge said thoughtfully. "There is *one* thing stronger than all the armies in the world."

"Which is…?"

"An idea whose time has come."

It began as a daring thought hatched at first by Oreta Cook. When she asked Marge to come into her office, Marge knew the time had arrived for "an idea."

As Oreta outlined what might be done, Marge's excitement grew. "We're going to buck the system," Oreta reminded. "In doing so, we'll suffer a lot of bruises. It's not going to be easy."

"No, but then the last ten years haven't been easy. Perhaps God made it this way to prepare me."

Oreta nodded in understanding. "It still hurts, doesn't it?"

"Not as much. The first day I came back here after Barry died, I couldn't believe how a crowded school could be so empty. Barry's memory was everywhere. His absence was overpowering. Once I began focusing on the other children a certain peace set in, somehow, I knew Barry was here in spirit, perhaps more now than when in the physical." Marge smiled softly. "Does that make sense?"

Oreta reached across her desk and touched Marge's hand. "Yes, it does. That's why I wanted to tell you my idea first."

"Idea? Or battle plan?"

It was a battle plan that began with Marge sending a serious letter asking all parents of the training center's students to attend a meeting at the Health Department. When the meeting took place, there was standing-room only. Marge took the podium. The room was stuffy as she scanned the sea of faces of those gathered. Most were there out of curiosity rather than commitment. All appeared alert and intelligent. "We're getting a new school," she said loudly and with confidence.

The crowd went wild with applause.

"The federal government is finally allocating some money?" someone asked.

"Nope," Marge responded.

"The county is?" another questioned.

"Nope," Marge called back.

There was a moment of silence as puzzlement turned smiles into frowns. Marge explained her strange response. "We're going to raise the money ourselves."

The crowd was a like a balloon suddenly pricked.

"We can't raise a million dollars!" came a disgruntled voice.

Marge stood firm. "Yes, we can. It's already out there. We simply need to find a way to direct it our way."

Amid a flurry of being told their idea was foolish to someone suggesting a bake sale, the truth was a million dollars was a tremendous amount of money—money that could only come from one major source: Uncle Sam.

Subsequent meetings were held with the most simplistic idea to the most absurd discussed. Letters were sent, petitions signed. Time after time, they were told that money was available with many requirements and restrictions. In the meantime, senators, representatives, and other government officials were contacted. At one point, Marge was twelve hours away from flying to Washington to lobby, when at the last minute, the decision was made not to go. They could have the money, *but* it could only be used in a slum area.

"We're already in the slums," Marge retaliated angrily. "What we want is *out* of the slums!"

Crushed but not defeated, the grant was refused. Their next battle line was closer to home: DeKalb County. Marge had already talked to local officials but had been politely wished well "with your federal pursuit."

Marge fortified her energy by silently repeating the motto, In God We Trust. And each time she did, she thought of Betty Jo and heard the words, *Grant me the courage to change the things I can...*

Finally, Marge was called to the office of Jack Sartain, acting head of the DeKalb County Health Department, which was the agency who administered the funds at the training center—in essence, the center's *big man on campus.*

"I've been thinking about your claims that these children deserve a decent school." Marge held her breath. "And I agree with you. I am ready to publicly join your side."

Marge screamed with joy. "You're the first official brave enough to take a stand!" She couldn't wait to tell Oreta about their first miracle.

Although the first public official to take a stand, Jack Sartain was not the last. The following day, she received a call from the chairman of the DeKalb County Commission, Bob Guhl. Miracles were happening, especially when Marge discovered that neither Jack nor Bob knew the other had made the same decision! With this ammunition, Oreta and Marge quickly laid out their next strategy. Since only Bob Guhl and not the other commissioners were supporting them, a guiding parent committee was formed consisting of Marge and two other mothers. The *head of the octopus* is what they called themselves.

Each commissioner was assigned a parent chairman and two other parents who would lobby the commissioners. These commissioners were constantly called at work, at home, met on the street, and were even pleaded with in their own kitchens. Every time a commissioner turned around, they found a parent pleading for a new school: "Our kids deserve a safe and decent school!" was the universal lament.

Not only was each arm of the octopus reaching far and deep, but the octopus itself created of itself. Eventually Commissioner Liane Levetan, a former special ed teacher, came out in support of the school as did Commissioners Robert Lanier, Walt Russell, and Bob Morris. The person they thought would be their biggest supporter was Commissioner Michael Izoff because he had a retarded son in the county workshop across the street from the center.

They were dead wrong.

"Izoff will only stand on our side if it helps *his* political career," was one mother's opinion. "His goal is to be chairman of DeKalb County. In order to win this seat, he must carry the south end of the county, which is predominately Black."

Izoff made his agenda crystal clear.

Since the center was about fifty-fifty Black and White, Izoff would support Marge's group *only* if the voters were given an "all-or-nothing" vote. It was decided that the only way to raise the 1.6 million needed was with a countywide bond referendum. Since several projects were presented, they wound up with five issues:

1. Training Center—1.6 million
2. Human Resources Center for South DeKalb—2.3 million (Izoff's pet project)
3. Upgrade DeKalb libraries—3.4 million
4. Arts Center in North DeKalb—1.5 million
5. County Road Improvements—11 million

The total came to approximately $20 million for twenty years, which meant The Training Center would cost $25.20 per year on a $40,000.00 home.

Marge grew more feverish in her dedication to see a decent school built for retarded children. Denny, inspired and proud of Marge, was also surprised by her metamorphosis from "passenger" to "driver." Not only was she taking charge of her life, but she was totally in control of its many extensions.

"Denny, will you go with me to meet with Izoff? I may have to beg him to support the program. If I do, I might need you there to catch me as I fall to my knees."

Michael Izoff listened to Marge's pleas with a certain aloofness.

When she finished, he reached over and touched the gold necklace Denny had given her for her birthday. It had only cost twenty dollars but apparently looked more expensive.

"Why don't you hock that?" Izoff asked sarcastically. "That'll give you a down payment for your school."

Shocked, Marge and Denny stared at each other in total disbelief. When they were alone, Marge asked Denny how it was possible for a politician to be so insensitive?

Denny's disgust was visible. "Marge, there are some politicians with such little sensitivity that they actually brag about getting their feeble old mom a job as a scrub woman at city hall!"

Marge couldn't help but laugh. "Yep, and there are some politicians who, if their voters were cannibals, would promise them missionaries for dinner."

Denny's eyes widened. Where had his sweet Marge gone? "I can't believe *you* said that."

"I didn't. Mencken said it years ago."

"Maybe Izoff should read Mencken."

"For what good? Politicians like Izoff would only wonder what dessert to offer up *with* the missionaries." Marge's voice turned serious. "Denny, our goal should be to make certain the voters are the missionaries and the cannibals are completely starved out."

*****

A mother's memory of her five-year-old son

"MOMMY, GUESS WHAT I FINDED OUT TODAY?"

"What, Barry?"

"I FINDED OUT THAT YOU SHOULDN'T JUMP OUT OF SOME KID'S TREEHOUSE HOLDIN' TO THE STRING OF BALLOON."

17

The Battle

Politicians are the same all over. They promise to
build a bridge even where there is no river.

—Khrushchev

Marge's concern over how Sherry was adapting to Barry's death was
greatly lessened after Sherry's third grade teacher showed her a paper
Sherry had written:

> Retarded kids are just like us, but some are
> blind and some can't talk or walk. But we should
> still not stare or laugh, for they can't help it that
> they're retarded. So you should treat them just
> like us kids.

Whenever the issues and climate became too heated and the
political in-fighting accelerated regarding the building of a new
school, Marge read Sherry's handwritten thought. It renewed her
strength, especially the part that said, *"So you should treat them just
like us kids."* Like Barry, all children deserved equal educational ben-
efits; none should be considered as throwaways.

With each standoff, emotions ran high. Liane Levetan invited
both sides to a meeting at her home. The lineup of those for the

training center versus those against it took on the complexion of "the Hatfields and the McCoys," with one side camped on the right, the other on the left.

After Oreta introduced Marge as president of the parents' group, Marge was the first to remind those gathered that a miracle had already taken place: the federal government had granted DeKalb County the land for a new training center on Peachtree Industrial Blvd., on the condition that funds for the building be raised within a given amount of time. This land had originally been the site of the old veterans hospital and was large enough to accommodate the kind of school needed. Oreta told the group how vandalism had worsened because of the current school's location in a high crime area. "What equipment that hasn't been stolen has been stored away. We're also very concerned for the safety of our staff. A staff member found a man in a classroom trying to pry open the lock on a desk. Parents have even been threatened. One mother was dragged down the sidewalk by a man when she refused to let go of her purse, while another staff member managed to push away a man who was forcing his way into her car."

Many in the group shook their heads.

"Although my staff and the parents are brave and very dedicated, it's reached the point that whenever they enter the building, they wonder if someone might be lurking in a dark corner. Lucidly this fear is lessened by the rewards received from seeing a totally unresponsive child learn to feed and dress himself. Still, it's tough trying to help one hundred and fifty mentally retarded people when equipment keeps disappearing and staff members have to spend their days cleaning up the debris vandals leave. Last week our staff spent the morning sweeping glass out of the gymnasium, covering broken windows, cleaning up from fire extinguishers that were thrown down hallways, and washing crude language off the walls. This takes away from helping the children. If we manage to raise money for new equipment, and if it's not taken from the school each day to be stored in someone's home, it's stolen. This is difficult when we're talking about air-conditioning units."

"The air-conditioning units are stolen?" someone asked.

"Yes. The present center has had televisions, stereos, small appliances, coffee machines, and audio equipment—anything loose including the children's books and toys, not to mention the daily occurence of rocks being thrown through windows," Oreta added sadly. "Vandals have been so bold that they've driven automobiles through doorways into the halls. Another time, while our mainte-nance man was away purchasing new locks for the doors, the build-ing was broken into while he was gone."

"Why not hire a full-time security guard or install a burglar alarm system?"

"Besides the fact that the building is condemned by the state fire marshal—who says we must vacate by July of 1977—hiring a full-time security guard is too expensive."

"The DeKalb Commission has already approved a burglar sys-tem for the center, but the system hasn't arrived yet," Liane Levetan advised.

"And even if it does arrive, I wouldn't be surprised if the system itself doesn't get stolen," a voice from the crowd suggested. "From what I've heard, spending money to guard the old school is like try-ing to cap a sewer that's already overflowing."

Uneasy laughter momentarily lightened the seriousness of the situation.

"And that's why we're here," Marge reminded everyone. "To build anew, not repair the unrepairable. Mini volcanoes and a water-fall in the restrooms are examples of the deteriorating condition of the school. This is because the pipes are in such poor shape that underground leaks give the appearance of tiny volcanic eruptions as water and fuel break the surface."

Once again people shook their heads.

"One restroom has been locked because of a massive leak in the ceiling," Marge continued. "Extreme amounts of water pour into the area during rainstorms."

"Conditions are dangerous," Oreta added. "Ceilings are falling down, walls are crumbling, floor tiles are missing, and the concrete is cracked with earth and rocks exposed. Electrical wiring is exposed and dangerous, making those rooms still in use subject to sudden fires. If there was a fire, there are not enough outside doors to get students out of classrooms. Heating pipes running under the floor in some classrooms are so hot they're melting the linoleum."

Liane Levetan looked at the mothers and fathers standing on both sides of the room, then said, "If you had children in this classroom, they'd burn themselves if they sat down on the floor. If these were normal children, they certainly wouldn't be expected to be in this kind of a building, would they?"

"So why not make repairs?" one father asked.

Marge looked at the man with disdain. "One major holdup in making the many needed repairs—beyond a cost exceeding $100,000 on a building not worth repairing—is political. The center is leased from the County Board of Education by the federal government. The board won't make any repairs since they're leasing the property to the government, and the government won't make any repairs because they don't own the property. And even if we managed to get beyond this immediate frustration, we'd still be in a crime-ridden area, thus our need is urgent. We can no longer accept that which is leftover and not wanted by those in our state, those who think of our handicapped children as being second-class citizens. If we're to be a nation with a heart, a nation who cares for *all* of its people, then we must make it possible for *every* child to receive an education in a school that's befitting a great nation. If we don't take care of all of our children, no matter what the nature of their finances, religion, or physical abilities, then we'll cease to be great. To deny any child equality because of physical restrictions is another form of slavery. Whether any American is forced to learn in a place that is not only substandard but condemned cannot be justified by its cost. What is the gain if in saving a few pennies, moral bankruptcy is underwritten?"

"We're talking county, not federal," a man interjected.

"Yes," Marge responded, "but a county is no more divided from its whole—the nation—than is one's arm separate from its body. Division of this sort renders ineffectiveness. DeKalb County must reflect the values of the nation it's a part of."

Applause was mingled with disgruntled sighs and angry head shaking. Scanning the faces of both sides of the crowd, Marge inhaled deeply before continuing. "The real division today isn't between those who want to spend and those who don't—it's between caring and noncaring, between equality and inequality. Its focus must be on the human element."

"Yes, but what good is a government that spends its money foolishly? Education has also been established so that those educated will someday *return* something back to society," one of the "McCoys" shouted.

"And are you all-wise enough to determine *which* of those educated will do the better job on the return trip? Would you have been willing to throw away a Hellen Keller because she was thought retarded and thus untrainable?"

A few in the crowd shuffled their feet uncomfortably; others lowered their eyes.

"The bottom line is we *have* to build a new training center. The building is falling apart and, as Oreta explained, has been condemned." Marge's voice filled with passion and sincerity. "We're in a crisis. You and the voters are our only ray of hope. You can make a difference by talking up the bond issue at your church, synagogue, civic club. You can urge your relatives, friends, and neighbors to get out and vote for a *new* training center. If you don't do this, there'll be no place for these special children after July of 1977. A new facility has already been proposed to meet the needs of these students and can be built on property owned by the federal government on Peachtree Industrial Blvd., the site of the old VA hospital."

"What's the new center going to do?"

Oreta answered that question. "Like the existing center, it will be designed to train the profoundly retarded how to live in a home environment. Each child is admitted regardless of his progress. Students are not required to meet any levels of learning. If a prospective student is in his twenties and not toilet trained, that doesn't matter at the center. However, the earlier in a child's development the center is able to reach him, the better. *Hopeless* is a word never used because we know each child has potential. The center is there to look for it. Sometimes one of the first things we have to do is untrain—to break habits that have been taught due to overpampering. Our students aren't allowed to become vegetables. They're made to function. Sometimes a child can ask for what he wants but has found that all he need do is grunt, thus that's all he does. Labels are then attached to the child, when in truth these children simply haven't been trained. They have no self-discipline."

"What's the cost to the parents?"

"The center's free. It also has an extended care program that begins at 7:00 a.m. before school actually starts and continues from 2:20 p.m. until 6:00 p.m. for working parents. Except for two weeks at Christmas, it carries out its program year-round. This is so as not to disrupt the continuity of the students' training. Its programs are designed to help both the student and the family and will accept any child denied acceptance to public school programs. The center's aim, if possible, is to move the student back into public school within a very carefully planned individual program."

A man rose from his chair and asked, "I thought there were programs already in place through the normal school system?"

"There are," Marge replied. "I need to stress that the center is *not* in competition with the public-school system. The DeKalb County School system is doing a great job with its programs for the handicapped. We're speaking of the child with an IQ less than thirty-five." She looked in the direction of Michael Izoff. "Sadly, there are those in our society who feel these people cannot be trained."

Michael Izoff looked away.

"What if a student at the center cannot be placed in a public-school program?"

"The center can make the child a more acceptable member of his family and community," Oreta responded quietly. "We're teaching our students to live in their homes, to be better citizens, to be able to care for themselves, to dress, feed and toilet train themselves, to get along with their peers. The center is now caring for and seeing progress in children and adults who cannot walk or talk, epileptic students, schizoid and autistic children, and students with numerous other handicaps. The *only* children the center does not accept are those who can find a place in public school programs."

Marge told the crowd a little about Barry. "Parents play a big role in the center's operation. Most of the time, parents come to the center frustrated and scarcely are able to face another day. I know, I've been there. Our TNT committee—Trials and Triumphs—meets regularly to help calm the frustrations and solve the problems often brought about by having a mentally retarded person in the family. Although we have no magic answers, this common bond helps alleviate the strain."

Oreta nodded. "The center also has a Parent Care Group made up of volunteer parents who are called upon day or night to help a family crisis. It's been used every month since its inception. All a parent has to do is call the center or me to get help."

"What happens to these people if they're not provided home environment training?"

"They're often institutionalized at an annual cost of over five times the cost of training. The new school, via a bond referendum, would cost the taxpayer only sixty-three cents per thousand a year based on ownership of a home valued at $40,000. Isn't that a small price to pay in order to help those who cannot help themselves?"

One of the "McCoys" stood. "You have our sympathy. But surely there must be other ways for funding besides a bond referendum?"

Marge felt her back stiffen. Didn't they know all the avenues that had been tried over the past few years? There certainly had been enough press. She had even written to President and Mrs. Jimmy Carter since special education was a favorite project of Mrs. Carter's. The end result was that fund allocations were being reviewed. But would funds come in time? "Of course we've attempted to raise funds by going through the appropriate channels, but to no avail. We began our initial fundraising project by a sale of homemade arts and crafts at a shopping plaza, and later a commitment for $360,000 was made by the County Commission when it was believed that nearly two million in federal funds was coming from the Economic Development Administration, funds now allocated to finance water line distribution throughout DeKalb."

"We explored *all* avenues," Liane Levetan underlined. "It often appeared that we were so close only to discover that those in power decided to use available funds elsewhere. It's imperative that the county get this project funded as soon as possible so that the land itself does not revert back to the federal government."

Michael Izoff drew to his feet. "Well, as the man before me said, you have our sympathy, Mrs. Glider. I also have a child who is retarded. *I* take care of his needs. I don't expect the taxpayer to do everything. Taxes should be used for that, which serves the most of us, not the least of us."

"We appreciate your sympathy, Mr. Izoff, which we've received a great deal of. But sympathy won't raise the 1.6 million needed for a new school. We wanted the voters to have five separate votes, one per issue. The other side wanted one vote only, all or nothing. To win, they needed to tie everything to the training center."

"No, of course, it won't. However, a bond referendum might be better served elsewhere. I'd suggest a more middle-of-the-road approach be taken."

Marge tilted her head. "And isn't the middle of the road where the White line is?"

Michael Izoff's brow arched. "Yes. Your point?"

Shrugging slightly, Marge's voice shaded with irony. "My point is, isn't the middle of the road the very worst place to drive?"

*****

A mother's memory of her five-year-old son

"MOMMY, GUESS WHAT I FINDED OUT TODAY?"

"What, Barry?"

"I FINDED OUT THAT I CAN SAY MY ABCs WITH MY EYES CLOSED."

18

Barry Reborn

Without victory there is no survival.

—Winston Churchill

The "project," as it was now called, became a case of trying to weave straw into gold, or if in fairy-tale terms rather than "once upon a time," it became "once upon a miracle."

As of January 1977, their group had contacted everyone from members of Congress to the White House to the media outlining the plight of the existing training center and the need for a new one. Knowing their project was competing for the same funds as other groups, it was repeatedly stressed that building a new center was in the long run less costly than institutionalizing a child. "It costs around $16,000 a year to keep a person in a state institution and only $3,000 a year to keep that same person in the community," Marge said so many times that the figures were burned in her brain.

Time was of the essence. On January 5, 1977, HEW had written to the Honorable Walter B. Russell, chairman of the Board of Commissioners: "We approved the plan which called for the completion of the training Center by fall of 1977. This was the last extension that will be granted for beginning utilization of the property for health purposes. A cursory on-site inspection of the 12.523 acre portion of the former VA Hospital was made this date. The inspection revealed that construction of the Training Center had not begun; therefore, can it be completed by November 1, 1977? This facility must be in use by that date to avoid title revestment of the property."

Three years of battling uphill and now they were faced with the demise of the property upon which to build a center they had no funds for. To Marge it appeared as though she faced another death sentence. "Denny, we *only* have nine months to do the impossible, nine months in which to see a miracle occur."

"Miracles *can* occur in nine months, Marge. Think about it. It takes nine months to create new life. Isn't the creation of new life the greatest miracle of all?"

Marge nodded. "I needed that," she acknowledged. "I also needed to be reminded that a new training center gives the child I carried for nine months a *reason for being*." She walked over to a table where a series of family photos sat. There were pictures with Barry *before* Hurlers and pictures with Barry *after* Hurlers. Turning, she smiled at Denny. "It's strange how life seems a series of balancing acts. We had two Barrys in our life, each for five years."

Denny looked at the photos with both pain and joy.

"Each had his own distinct personality," Marge said, then smiled. "When God called Barry home, He had to open His arms wide enough for two little boys living in one body."

"And which Barry do you miss?" Denny asked.

Marge looked at Denny with a thoughtful expression. "I miss them both, Denny. And it's for both that I'll see this new center built. *In God We trust,* I swear I will."

Elliott Levitas, Georgia's member of the House of Representatives, went to bat for them by contacting the Department of Health, Education, and Welfare to urge them to grant an extension on the deadline for utilization of the property so it would not revert back to the federal government. He ended his letter by stating, "I can think of no other way that this property could be better used than for this training center. I am also looking into other possible sources of funds."

Miracles were happening. Newspapers, radio, and television began calling Marge and Oreta for interviews. The coverage was sensational. Marge was being called "Barry's Mom." Yet with each step taken in support of the project, there were hurts that always ran quite deep. "Last night at my home, I received a telephone call," Marge told one interviewer. "It was from a man who refused to identify himself. He had read one of the news articles and was furious that I wanted to waste the taxpayer's money on such a useless project. He shouted that these kids would never amount to anything, and he wasn't going to waste his money. Then he hung up."

"How do you maintain your focus and your strength?" the interviewer asked.

"I look at a silver dollar that I sometimes carry with me. It says *In God We Trust*. And," Marge added, "I remember the words of a special lady, an ang…" She almost said the word *angel* but decided doing so might sound bizarre. She had the feeling that although most people believed angels existed, she was uncertain of the level of this sort of faith. Once again, recalling the words of Mencken who had written, "Faith was an illogical belief in the occurrence of the improbable," she knew that keeping quiet was best. After all, there were more times than not that she also questioned the possibility of *who* Betty Jo was, *why* Betty Jo had been in a bed next to her in a maternity ward without having given birth, why the telephone number and address she had given proved to be invalid, and *why* she had known beforehand that Marge needed to be prepared for having a retarded child.

Whoever Betty Jo was and *why* she had come into her life, Marge knew from the depths of her soul she had been heavenly sent.

And that was enough, more than enough.

Angels came in many forms. Marge reached into her purse for a card upon which was printed the poem "Footprints in the Sand." During Barry's long illness and after his leaving, she had received numerous copies of the famed poem. She showed it to the interviewer. "I don't know who wrote this, but these words are a constant reminder that we are never alone, that He is always carrying us. And then I remember a little boy with wide blue eyes who wanted to leave his own footprints in the sands of time and who wanted so desperately to live the life of any little boy." Marge was now able to smile when remembering Barry. "Barry loved the holidays. He was four, and it was the week before Christmas. We had our tree up, and there were already gifts under it. He knew Christmas was for giving, so whenever the doorbell rang, he'd run to the tree and present anyone with a gift as they came in the door. We had quite a time convincing him *not* to give them all away!"

"Is it hard remembering?" the interviewer asked.

"Not anymore. Barry was our gift from God. A woman I met in the hospital when Barry was born told me that retarded children are very special, that they are here for a reason." Marge drew her shoulders back. "No child should ever be considered a 'throwaway.'"

Another miracle occurred when the deadline for usage of the land was extended. Although it required construction to begin by November 1, 1977, the center had until November 1, 1978, for its completion. The bond referendum would be presented to the voters in June not on an "all or nothing" basis but as five separate items.

This in itself was a monumental victory. Marge was only sorry she couldn't see Michael Izoff's expression when he learned that his viewpoint was very unpopular.

If their project was voted in and they were awarded the 1.6 million, they would have only four months in which to have the building plans ready for that first shovel of dirt. But considering it took nine months to see a new life to completion, what was four months in the design of a building?

Media coverage accelerated with headlines reading:

> 20 million bond issue election called for June 14 spotlight on the training center
>
> One of the major questions surround placement of the DeKalb Training Center for the profoundly retarded on the June 14 bond issue ballot is a tough one for Dekalb voters. More importantly, it is: Can DeKalb County afford *not* to approve the training center?

Among the many interviews, the one that seemed to strike the deepest chord with voters was the one that came from Marge's voice:

> On June 14 every DeKalb County voter will be asked to vote on the DeKalb Training Center for the profoundly retarded to approve bonds to provide funds to construct a new facility as the present school has been condemned as of July 1, 1977. These students have for too long been denied their rights as citizens and the right to develop into productive human beings. Until you have personally experienced the hurt and frustration as a parent and then to find hope for a brighter future, do not judge us but help us! Vote yes on the DeKalb Training Center for the profoundly retarded.

June 14, 1977, may have been heralded in as just another hot summer day in Georgia, another Tuesday where traffic backed up, where city streets sizzled, and where children, glad that school was out, played in parks.

June 14 was anything but normal for Marge and Denny. It was a do-or-die situation. After casting their votes, they returned home for the long wait. Although Marge talked to Oreta a dozen times on the telephone, neither wanted to openly state that this day was the climax to all of their dreams.

Victory or failure?

An election party was planned at a local restaurant for later that evening where everyone on the ballot would be together in order to keep track of the vote. Marge prayed that this gathering would also be a victory party for the training center.

And for Barry.

June 14 was also Denny's thirty-eighth birthday. "I know the vote will pass," Marge kept promising herself as much as Denny. "It will be Barry's birthday gift to you."

Never before had the ritual of talking and walking been so tedious. Marge felt every nerve throbbing in her body. She was trying to ignore the day itself and concentrate on Sherry and baking a birthday cake for Denny. She had no idea why she kept peering out the kitchen window. It was as if to do so would hurry up a day that was moving incredibly slow. Despite her attempts at turning her attention elsewhere, she kept asking herself: Had she worked hard enough? Had she done everything possible to get the plight of the center to the public? And if so, would their county care *enough?*

Finally, they left for the restaurant in order to join their group in a reserved room. The other groups were located in other parts of the restaurant hoping their issues would also win.

The votes were tallied. Everyone held their breath.

"We won!" Denny shouted. "We passed four to one! The other issues were all defeated four to one!"

While everyone in the room went wild with hysterical joy, Marge lowered her head. "*Thank you,*" she whispered.

A struggle was over. Although Marge was listening to what Denny was saying, and although there were many things about this moment that needed to be vocalized, she was not quite ready to believe the magnitude of their victory.

"You won," Denny repeated softy as he smoothed back a strand of hair from her eyes. "*You won...*"

Marge looked at Denny with disbelief on her face. "*We* won, Denny. All of us won: Oreta, Liane, the parents, the children, and Barry—especially Barry."

The architect selected was Garland Reynolds from Gainesville, Georgia. He was not only an excellent designer but was sensitive to the fact that the design of the center should have staff and parent involvement. This time around, the meetings were one of joy and peace rather than anger and war.

Garland was given limitless ideas and suggestions and, amazingly, was able to incorporate just about everything in the final design. The 38,000 square-foot training center, designed to provide a contemporary noninstitutional learning environment, was to have sixteen classrooms divided into pods around a central support facility and activity core, which could serve as a multipurpose room with audio-visual capabilities. Able to accommodate approximately two hundred students of varying ages and skill levels, the center would meet a wide range of educational needs such as personal grooming, health care, and household training as well as physical recreation and therapy. In addition to year-round classroom instruction, the center would provide music, speech, transportation, extended care services for working parents, hot lunches, parent involvement programs, counseling and referral services, and psychiatric and medical consultation. Windows would be moderately sized and secured. There would be specially designed toilet facilities. Kitchen facilities would have a central dining area. Outside, trees would be saved wherever possible, and there would be 100 square feet of fenced area per child, with ample parking available for staff and visitors.

During a reception at the Board of Health, its director, Dr. Gunar Bohan, asked if she could speak privately to Marge. Puzzled, Marge nodded. When they were alone, she told Marge, "I've received a petition signed by all the parents at the training center requesting that the new school be named *The Barry Glider Memorial Center*. This petition has been approved. It was a unanimous vote by the parents and also by the DeKalb County Commission."

Marge was so shocked that she felt her knees go weak. It was as if Barry had been reborn, and in a sense, he had. In the larger scheme of things, Barry's existence was to mean so much to so many.

His existence was eternal.

On October 13, 1977, ground was broken for the new center, a center that would—four years after his leaving—honor a little boy named Barry.

The groundbreaking was covered by many of the same powers who had banded together to see that one little boy's "footprints in the sands of time" would indeed make a difference. The official ground-breaking program stated:

> Like Barry, the concept for training the
> severely and profoundly retarded was young.
> Together, their growth was not easy and their

lives were filled with tears, frustrations, hopes and joys which are necessary for understanding and achievement. For parents, teachers, and friends alike, this new facility represents a dream come true—a dream embodied in each and every student it will serve—a dream made a reality through hard work, dedication, and brotherhood—and a dream for future accomplishments.

They had embraced the *courage to change what they could.* Their dream had come true, ironically in the same city that gave rise to a great man who said, "I have a dream…"

As Marge, Denny, and Sherry stood clasping the hand of the other, a neighbor came to them and whispered, "I never understood *why* you wouldn't put Barry in an institution. But after seeing all of this, after seeing how many lives Barry has touched, I understand."

Marge also possessed understanding. Little by little one of the pieces of life's puzzles fell into place. She now *knew* the answer to why? Barry's short life, even his suffering, had been for a reason. God had used her through her love for Barry to help other children have a better life. God's plan was far larger than any of their plans, yet God needed His children to work through. Through God, ordinary people *could* accomplish the extraordinary. She had tried to leave God, tried to incite His anger, tried to punish and dismiss Him. What she had forgotten was that He had chosen *not* to leave her.

As she looked heavenward, a gigantic ray of sun enveloped her, bathing her in a warmth that reached into her soul. The sun's rays took on the dimensions of a cross. Within its light, she heard one angelic voice that whispered, *Live your life by the motto on this coin,* and then a second more powerful voice that said, *He is with Me.*

*****

A mother's memory of her five-year-old son

"MOMMY, GUESS WHAT I FINDED OUT TODAY?"

"What, Barry?"

"I finded out that when you stick your finger in the peanut butter jar and lick your fingers, the peanut butter tastes better."

Because of people like Marge Glider—who fought so hard for the rights of retarded children—PUBLIC LAW 94142 changed the education system in our nation.

It is now mandatory for public school systems to educate *all* children from six to twenty-one years of age in the "least restrictive environment."

Dekalb County was able to remove Barry Gilder from the school system because there was no law mandating public education. A law was passed—Public Law 94142—in the seventies which made free public education a right of every child.

Since Public Law 94142, The Training Center, federally funded, serves children from birth until six, then receives the adults back at twenty-one until death if necessary.

Addendum

Unfortunately, history repeated itself. Sherry had three sons and her middle son inherited this genetic disease. Due to progress in testing, it was discovered that both boys had Hunter's syndrome instead of Hurler's, as we had been told. That is why Sherry's Hurler tests showed negative, that she was not a carrier. The doctors were looking for the wrong disease. Her other two sons are now grown and the picture of health and happiness.

*****

A mother's memory of her five-year-old son

"Mommy, guess what I finded out today?"

"What, Barry?"

"I finded out that peanut butter has the word pea in it so I can eat that with my mashed 'tatoes 'stead of peas, right?"

Heaven's Very Special Child
A meeting was held quite far from earth,
"It's time again for another birth,"
Said the angels to the Lord above.
"This special child will need much love.
His progress may seem very slow;
Accomplishments-he may not show.
And he'll require extra care,
From the folks he meets down there.
He may not run or laugh or play:
His thoughts might seem quite far away.
In many ways he won't adapt,
And he'll be known as handicapped.
So let's be careful where he's sent;
We want his life to be content.
Please, Lord, find the parents who
Will do a special job for you.
They will not realize right away,
The leading role they're asked to play.
But with this child sent from above,
Comes stronger faith and richer love.
And soon they'll know the privilege given
In caring for these Gifts from Heaven.
Their precious charge, so meek and mild,
Is Heaven's Very Special Child."

Edna Massimilla

The above poem was a gift from Denny to Marge the year after Barry's death. Done in calligraphy by a priest, it hangs in a special place in their home always touching family and friends who visit.

*****

158

A mother's memory of her five-year-old son

"MOMMY, GUESS WHAT I FINDED OUT TODAY?"

"What, Barry?"

"I FINDED OUT THAT IF YOU MAKE AN ICE CUBE SANDWICH, YOUR BREAD GETS ALL SOGGY."

Proposed New DeKalb County Training Center for the Mentally Retarded to Receive New Name in Memory of Former Student

by Dr. Gunar N. Bohan, MD, MPH
Date: 2/28/77

When Barry Glider, age 8, was enrolled in the DeKalb Training Center in 1972, there was a sigh of relief from his parents, Mr. and Mrs. Dennis Glider. For several years they had experienced the frustration of being turned away by special education classes within the public school system in their efforts to find a training program for their young, mentally retarded son. In 1969, however, the DeKalb County Health Department opened the doors of a revolutionary new program designed especially to meet the needs of children and adults like Barry.

The Gliders were greatly relieved and demonstrated their appreciation by becoming active members of the Center's Parent Group.

In September, 1973 Mrs. Marge Glider was installed as the President of the Parent Group and then, in October, tragedy touched the Glider's lives, as well as the lives of parents and staff at the center. Barry, now age 9, succumbed to a fatal, progressively degenerative condition known as Hurler's Syndrome.

In spite of their loss, and with the encouragement of the Center's parents and staff, the Gliders remained very active within both the Training Center and the community in working toward helping the mentally retarded citizens of DeKalb County.

Mrs. Glider has been elected President of the Parent Group every year since, and has fought long and hard to improve the quality of services available to the severely and profoundly retarded.

The past several years had been most difficult for the DeKalb Training Center, as many disappointments have threatened the existence of this program. The old school building, in which the program is housed, has been under fire by local and state officials for failure to meet minimum Life and Safety Code requirements. The longtime dream of seeing a new facility constructed seemed a nightmare when the County learned that their grant application for Federal Public Works monies with which to construct the new facility, was turned down. Mrs. Glider has been actively involved since the beginning and, even in the face of all these disappointments, has remained undaunted in her commitment to see her dream, and that of many other parents, become a reality.

A bright note in the story of the DeKalb Training Center occurred Friday, February 25, 1977, when Dr. Gunar Bohan, the Director of the DeKalb County Health Department, in a surprise announcement, informed Mrs. Glider of the County Board of Health's decision to rename a new training center the "Barry Glider Memorial Center of DeKalb County." Dr. Bohan was approached in October 1976 by members of the current Center's Parent Group, supported by County Commissioner Liane Levetan and Center Director, Oreta Cook, with the request to rename the new facility which, at that time, had seemed assured. In their written request, the group cited Mrs. Glider's "love and devotion toward the mentally retarded...even after the untimely death of her own child." Dr. Bohan responded by promising to submit the request to the Board of Health, and commented that this action would "seem to be a most appropriate manner in which to honor someone who has devoted five years of service."

Dr. Bohan's sentiments seemed to be shared by all the members of the Board present at their February 24th meeting. Chairman Gary S. Cutini., Dr. Stanley P. Aldridge, President of the DeKalb County Medical Society, Mr. Walter B. Russell, Jr., Chairman of the DeKalb County Board of Commissioners, and Mayor W. B. Malone unanimously voted to rename the proposed new facility.

Mrs. Glider was visibly moved by the announcement as she had not been aware of the original request. In a later comment Mrs. Glider stated that the action by the Board of Health was "a total shock" and that she felt "extremely humble" by their decision. Dr. Bohan voiced her personal feelings of respect for Mrs. Glider and her support of the construction of a new facility which Dr. Bohan stated she hoped "to see realized in the near future."

The proposal for renaming the new Center will be brought before the DeKalb County Board of Commissioners who have a final authority for approval.

Epilogue

With the odds of having another child with Hunter's syndrome being almost 50/50, Marge and Dennis regrettably did not have any more children. They felt that the outcome was too uncertain and were afraid of history repeating itself. Marge was always grateful to God, however, that they had been blessed with a healthy daughter born to them prior to their son's diagnosis. She was a gift from God.

Since their daughter was raised as an only child, she understood the loneliness of not having any siblings. Therefore she promised herself that she would never have just one child. When she was twenty-four, she met and married a wonderful Christian man and was blessed with three beautiful sons.

When her middle son was two, there were some things they began to notice regarding his health. This brought up many questions. After taking him to a geneticist at Emory University in Atlanta, he was diagnosed with Hunter's syndrome. This led us to search for Barry's medical records at Shands Teaching Hospital in Gainesville, Florida, where Barry had been treated. This is when we learned that Barry had actually been misdiagnosed and it was a Hunter's syndrome instead of a Hurler's syndrome. It is simply a different enzyme but each one has different characteristics. It is amazing what the destruction of one tiny missing enzyme can do to the human body. Her son lost his battle after a fourteen-year struggle with this devastating disease. The blessing in this story is that females are the carrier of the gene. After two generations, this affliction can finally end in their family.

Today there is ongoing research working with Hunter and Hurler patients. There are enzyme trials being held that they have found to produce some positive results with the health issues these patients face. However, at this time, the replacement therapy has not been able to restore or prevent this disease from its destruction.

DEKALB COUNTY BOARD OF COMMISSIONERS

Walter B. Russell, Jr., Chairman

William A. Williams   Jim Patterson
Liane Levetan   Manuel J. Maloof
Robert E. Lanier   Brince H. Manning, III

DEKALB COUNTY HEALTH DEPARTMENT

Gary S. Cutini,
Chairman, Board of Health
Gunar N. Bohan, M.D., M.P.H.,
Director, DeKalb Co. Health Dept.
James E. Mallory,
Director, Division of Mental Health/Mental Retardation
Oreta C. Cook,
Director, Training Center
Marge J. Glider,
President, Parents Group

GROUNDBREAKING COMMITTEE

Oreta Cook   Peggy Maier
Marge Glider   Kay Payne
Karen Harkins   Fran Sheats
Liane Levetan   Jim J. Wilder

ARCHITECT:
M. Garland Reynolds & Partners
CONTRACTOR:
Rogers Construction Company
CONSTRUCTION MANAGEMENT:
J. William Goodhew, Warner & Associates

This is to acknowledge our appreciation to the voters of DeKalb County for making this Center a reality.

DeKalb County Board of Commissioners
Parent Group, DeKalb Training Center
Staff, DeKalb Training Center

GROUNDBREAKING
THE BARRY GLIDER MEMORIAL BUILDING
10:00 A.M. October 13, 1977

* * * * * *

Master of Ceremonies .... Fran Sheats
Commissioners Office Administrator,
DeKalb County

* * *

Dedication Scripture .... Reverend Martin D. Gable
St. Martin In-the-Fields
Episcopal Church
Prayer of Invocation............................. Reverend Wray Ivey
First Baptist Church of Swainsboro
Introduction of Special Guests
Address .... Dr. Stephen Cornett
Director of Handicapped Individuals,
Division of Human Developmental
Services, HEW
Expression of Thanks .... Gunar N. Bohan, M.D., M.P.H.,
Director, DeKalb County Health Department
Benediction .... Dr. Ken Nishimura
Department of Philosophy
Oglethorpe University
Official Groundbreaking .... Walter B. Russell, Jr., Chairman,
DeKalb County Board of Commissioners
Brince H. Manning, Jr., Past Chairman,
DeKalb County Board of Commissioners
W. Douglas Skelton, M.D., Commissioner,
Georgia Department of Human Resources
Dr. James H. Hinson, Jr.,
Superintendent, DeKalb County
School System

BARRY GLIDER MEMORIAL CENTER

OF

DEKALB COUNTY

CONSTRUCTION MANAGER
WARNER & ASSOCIATES, INC.

ARCHITECT
M. GARLAND REYNOLDS & PARTNERS

GENERAL CONTRACTORS
ROGERS CONSTRUCTION CO.

BOARD OF COMMISSIONERS
WALTER B. RUSSELL, JR. CHAIRMAN
WILLIAM A. WILLIAMS
LIANE LEVETAN
ROBERT E. LANIER
JAMES M. PATTERSON
BRINCE H. MANNING, III
MANUEL J. MALOOF

The DeKalb Training Center for the
Profoundly Mentally Handicapped
DeKalb County, Georgia

MARGE GLIDER

DEKALB COUNTY
BOARD OF COMMISSIONERS

ACTION AGENDA ITEM ABSTRACT

MEETING DATE August 9, 1977

Action Agenda

Item No. **5**

Subject: Training Center for the Profoundly Retarded -- Proposed Name

Department: **Commissioner's Office**	Public Hearing: _____ yes _X_ no
Attachment(s): **None**	Information Contact: **Chairman Russell**
	Phone Number: **371-2881**

Previous submission as Preliminary Item No. **5** distributed on **July 26, 1977** .

Purpose: To consider naming the Training Center for the Profoundly
Retarded the "Barry Glider Memorial Center of DeKalb County,"
in accordance with recommendation of the Board of Health.

Need: To provide identification for the Center.

Impact: Approval would honor a boy who was enrolled in the Training
Center at the time of his death and whose mother has devoted
a great deal of time and effort toward helping the profoundly
retarded.

Recommendation(s): Name the new Training Center for the Profoundly Retarded
the "Barry Glider Memorial Center of DeKalb County," in
accordance with recommendation of the Board of Health.

ELLIOTT H. LEVITAS
4th District, Georgia

WASHINGTON OFFICE:
329 Cannon House Office Building
Washington, D.C. 20515
(202) 225-4272

HOME OFFICE:
141 East Trinity Place
Decatur, Georgia 30030
(404) 377-1717

Congress of the United States
House of Representatives
Washington, D.C. 20515

PUBLIC WORKS AND
TRANSPORTATION COMMITTEE
SUBCOMMITTEES:
AVIATION
SURFACE TRANSPORTATION
PUBLIC BUILDINGS AND GROUNDS
INVESTIGATIONS AND REVIEW

GOVERNMENT OPERATIONS
COMMITTEE
SUBCOMMITTEES:
COMMERCE, CONSUMER AND
MONETARY AFFAIRS
INTERGOVERNMENTAL
RELATIONS AND HUMAN
RESOURCES

June 29, 1977

Ms. Marge Glider
397 Fond du Lac Drive
Stone Mountain
Georgia 30088

Dear Ms. Glider:

Those of us who live in DeKalb County are grateful
for your leadership in bringing about the successful
bond referendum for the DeKalb Training Center.

The passage of the bond issue is a beacon of
hope for the many persons who so desperately need
these facilities.

With best personal regards, I am

Very truly yours,

Elliott H. Levitas
Member of Congress

EHL:pr

DEKALB'S MENTALLY RETARDED CHILDREN AND ADULTS NEED YOUR HELP!

1. The DeKalb Training Center is the only school serving profoundly and severely retarded children and adults in the entire county. *Bus service is provided throughout the county.*

2. The center offers the alternative of a community based program versus institutionalization to more than 150 families having mentally retarded children. *Parents, sisters, etc.*

3. The present facility has been condemned by the State Fire Marshal and will be closed on July 1, 1977.

Vote YES on the June 14 bond referendum for construction of a new training center to serve the mentally retarded citizens of our county.

5. *The center operates 12 months a year, 5 days a week, from 7:00 AM to 6:00 P.M. This extended day allows parents to work and they provide a higher quality of life for their families.*

6. *Services provided by the center average approximately $3,000 per year per student compared to over $13,000 to $16,000 per year at state institutions.*

7. *Operating expenses are provided by state and federal governments, there are no county funds involved in the present operation.*

A new school designed especially to meet the needs of these students would cost the taxpayer only 63¢ a year based on ownership of a home valued at $40,000.

8. *The property for the new building has been donated by the federal government but it will revert back to the government if not used by Nov., 1978.*

9. *Architectural plans are completed and ready for construction.*

10. *In summary, the training center provides services for profoundly retarded citizens of all ages. (infants - adults.) These citizens are not eligible for training in the public school system.*

PAID FOR BY CONCERNED CITIZENS OF DEKALB COUNTY

$1.26 - $65,00 Home

Don't our kids deserve a decent chance of a quality education with their families? We were fortunate

Proposed New DeKalb County Training Center for the Mentally
Retarded to Receive New Name in Memory of Former Student

by Dr. Gunar N. Bohan, M.D., M.P.H.
Date: 2/28/77

When Barry Glider, age 8, was enrolled in the DeKalb Training Center in 1972,
there was a sigh of relief from his parents, Mr. and Mrs. Dennis Glider. For
several years they had experienced the frustration of being turned away by
special education classes within the public school system in their efforts
to find a training program for their young, mentally retarded son. In 1969,
however, the DeKalb County Health Department opened the doors of a revolutionary
new program designed especially to meet the needs of children and adults
like Barry.

The Gliders were greatly relieved and demonstrated their appreciation by
becoming active members of the Center's Parent Group.

In September, 1973 Mrs. Marge Glider was installed as the President of the
Parent Group and then, in October, tragedy touched the Glider's lives,
as well as the lives of parents and staff at the center. Barry, now age 9,
succumbed to a fatal, progressively degenerative condition known as Hurler's
Syndrome.

In spite of their loss, and with the encouragement of the Center's parents
and staff, the Gliders remained very active within both the Training Center
and the community in working toward helping the mentally retarded citizens
of DeKalb County.

Mrs. Glider has been elected President of the Parent Group every year since,
and has fought long and hard to improve the quality of services available
to the severely and profoundly retarded.

The past several years have been most difficult for the DeKalb Training
Center, as many disappointments have threatened the existence of this
program. The old school building, in which the program is housed, has been
under fire by local and state officials for failure to meet minimum Life
and Safety Code requirements. The long time dream of seeing a new facility
constructed seemed a nightmare when the County learned that their grant
application for Federal Public Works monies with which to construct the
new facility, was turned down. Mrs. Glider has been actively involved since
the beginning and, even in the face of all these disappointments, has remained
undaunted in her committment to see her dream, and that of many other parents,
become a reality.

A bright note in the story of the DeKalb Training Center occurred Friday,
February 25, 1977, when Dr. Gunar Bohan, the Director of the DeKalb County
Health Department, in a surprise announcement, informed Mrs. Glider of the
County Board of Health's decision to rename a new training center the
"Barry Glider Memorial Center of DeKalb County". Dr. Bohan was approached
in October 1976 by members of the current Center's Parent Group, supported
by County Commissioner Liane Levetan and Center Director, Oreta Cook, with

the request to rename the new facility which, at that time, had seemed
assured. In their written request, the group cited Mrs. Glider's "love
and devotion toward the mentally retarded......even after the untimely
death of her own child". Dr. Bohan responded by promising to submit the
request to the Board of Health, and commented that this action would
"seem to be a most appropriate manner in which to honor someone who has
devoted five years of service".

Dr. Bohan's sentiments seemed to be shared by all the members of the Board
present at their February 24th meeting. Chairman Gary S. Cutini, Dr. Stanley
P. Aldridge, President of the DeKalb County Medical Society, Mr. Walter B.
Russell, Jr., Chairman of the DeKalb County Board of Commissioners, and
Mayor W. B. Malone unanimously voted to rename the proposed new facility.

Mrs. Glider was visibly moved by the announcement as she had not been
aware of the original request. In a later comment Mrs. Glider stated that
the action by the Board of Health was "a total shock" and that she felt
"extremely humble" by their decision. Dr. Bohan voiced her personal feelings
of respect for Mrs. Glider and her support of the construction of a new
facility which Dr. Bohan stated she hoped "to see realized in the near
future".

The proposal for renaming the new Center will be brought before the DeKalb
County Board of Commissioners who have a final authority for approval.

From
Great Aunt Thursa

From Betty Jo
Ramsey at Birth

Our motto in
life

who said
"the best things in life are free"?

item or service*	1963	cost
Maternity Clothes		150.00
Doctor		200.00
Hospital		150.00
Pediatrician		25.00
Orthopedic Surgeon		20.00
Baby Clothes		
Corrective Shoes		12.00

maternity clothes · layette · bassinet · GRIB · vitamins · pills · PILLS · PILLS · new hat · FLOWERS · REDECORATE · bathinet · BOTTLES · DOCTOR · HOSPITAL · PEDIATRIC

baby scales · mother's helper · BLANKETS · new hair-do · AFTER-BIRTH CLOTHES · washing machine · DRYER · baby buggy · DOG · cat · HORSE

NEW ADDITION TO HOUSE · TOYS · rocking chair · BABY RECORD BOOK · CHAMPAGNE FOR CELEBRATION · CIGARS · candy

* all things pertinent to my birth, Mom!

100

Barry   Barry

E E E E   E

F F F F   F

H H H H   H

I I I I   I

Barry would not finish his writing today

Barry   Barry   I

E E F E   E

F F F F   F

H H H H   H

About the Author

Marge Glider grew up between Florida and Michigan and earned her degree in English from Florida Southern College. She was a major proponent for special-needs children in the 1970s and went to battle against the establishment of the times to ensure equality for all. Her passion came from having a special-needs son with a rare genetic disease. Today she lives with her husband of fifty-nine years outside of Atlanta. Her daughter and son-in-law live nearby, and she has enjoyed being an active grandparent with her three grandsons. Marge and her husband are very active in their church, and if she isn't traveling, she can be found many afternoons on the tennis court. She is pleased to share their story and the legacy that was left to help so many other children.

CPSIA information can be obtained
at www.ICGtesting.com
Printed in the USA
LVHW111611070521
686791LV00005B/462